ACTS

The Good News of the *Holy Spirit*

A Guided Discovery for Groups and Individuals

Kevin Perrotta

LOYOLA PRESS.
A JESUIT MINISTRY
Chicago

LOYOLA PRESS.
A JESUIT MINISTRY

3441 N. Ashland Avenue
Chicago, Illinois 60657
(800) 621-1008
www.loyolapress.com

Imprimatur
Most Reverend Raymond E. Goedert,
  M.A., S.T.L., J.C.L.
Vicar General
Archdiocese of Chicago
June 22, 2000

Nihil Obstat
Reverend Michael Mulhall, O.Carm.
Censor Deputatus
June 20, 2000

The *Nihil Obstat* and *Imprimatur* are official declarations that a book is free of doctrinal and moral error. No implication is contained therein that those who have granted the *Nihil Obstat* and *Imprimatur* agree with the content, opinions, or statements expressed.

The Scripture quotations contained herein are from the New Revised Standard Version Bible: Catholic Edition, copyright © 1993 and 1989 by the Division of Christian Education of the National Council of the Churches of Christ in the U.S.A. Used by permission. All rights reserved. Subheadings in Scripture quotations have been added by Kevin Perrotta.

The Latin text of *Veni, Sancte Spiritus* (p. 21) can be found in Matthew Britt, ed., *The Hymns of the Breviary and Missal* (New York: Benziger Brothers, 1924). Translation by Kevin Perrotta.

Catherine de Hueck Doherty's quotation (p. 33) is from her book *Fragments of My Life* (Notre Dame, Ind.: Ave Maria Press, 1979).

A Latin rendering of St. Ephrem's commentary on Acts (p. 45) can be found in Frederick C. Conybeare, "The Commentary of Ephrem on Acts," in F. J. Foakes Jackson and Kirsopp Lake, eds., *The Beginnings of Christianity*, pt. 1, *The Acts of the Apostles*, vol. 3, *The Text of Acts* (London: Macmillan and Co., 1925). Translation by Kevin Perrotta.

Cardinal Léon Joseph Suenens's prayer (p. 56) is translated by Louise M. Perrotta. A French version is available in Karl-Heinz Fleckenstein, *Pour l'Eglise de demain: conversation avec le cardinal Suenens* (Paris: Nouvelle Cité, 1979).

Hope Medical Clinic, directed by Daniel Heffernan, M.D., can be contacted at 103 Arnet St., Ypsilanti, MI 48197, and at www.comnet.org/hopeclinic.

A Latin version of St. John Chrysostom's homilies on Acts (p. 69) can be found in J.-P. Migne, ed., *Patrologia Graeca*, vol. 60 (Paris, 1862). Translation by Kevin Perrotta.

The translation of the excerpt from *The Decree on the Apostolate of the Laity* (p. 80) is by Kevin Perrotta.

Interior design by Kay Hartmann/Communique Design
Illustration by Charise Mericle Harper

ISBN-13: 978-0-8294-1448-6
ISBN-10: 0-8294-1448-7

Printed in the United States of America
17 18 19 20 21 22 23 Bang 18 17 16 15 16 14 13

Contents

How to Use This Guide

You might compare this booklet to a short visit to a national park. The park is so large that you could spend months, even years, getting to know it. But a brief visit, if carefully planned, can be enjoyable and worthwhile. In a few hours you can drive through the park and pull over at a handful of sites. At each stop you can get out of the car, take a short trail through the woods, listen to the wind blowing in the trees, get a feel for the place.

In this booklet we'll drive through the Acts of the Apostles, making half a dozen stops along the way. At those points we'll proceed on foot, taking a leisurely walk through the selected passages. The readings have been chosen to take us to the heart of the book's message.

After each discussion we'll get back in the car and take the highway to the next stop. "Between Discussions" pages summarize the portions of Acts that we will pass along the way.

This guide provides everything you need to explore Acts of the Apostles in six discussions—or to do a six-part exploration on your own. The introduction on page 6 will prepare you to get the most out of your reading. The weekly sections feature key passages from Acts, with explanations that highlight what these words mean for us today. Equally important, each section supplies questions that will launch you into fruitful discussion, helping you both to explore Acts for yourself and learn from one another. If you're using the booklet by yourself, the questions will spur your personal reflection.

Each discussion is meant to be a *guided discovery*.

Guided. None of us is equipped to read the Bible without help. We read the Bible *for* ourselves but not *by* ourselves. Scripture was written to be understood and applied in and with the Church. So each week "A Guide to the Reading," drawing on the work of both modern biblical scholars and Christian writers of the past, supplies background and explanations. The guide will help you grasp the book's message. Think of it as a friendly park ranger who points out noteworthy details and explains what you're looking at so you can appreciate things for yourself.

Discovery. The purpose is for *you* to interact with Acts. "Questions for Careful Reading" is a tool to help you dig into the book and examine it carefully. "Questions for Application" will help you consider what Acts means for your life here and now. Each week concludes with an "Approach to Prayer" section that helps you respond to God's Word. Supplementary "Living Tradition" and "Saints in the Making" sections offer the thoughts and experiences of Christians past and present in order to show you what Acts has meant to others—so that you can consider what it might mean for you.

How long are the discussion sessions? We've assumed you will have about an hour and a half when you get together. If you have less time, you'll find that most of the elements can be shortened somewhat.

Is homework necessary? You will get the most out of the discussions if you read the weekly material in advance of each meeting. But if participants are not able to prepare, have someone read the "What's Happened" and "Guide to the Reading" sections aloud to the group at the points where they occur in the weekly material.

What about leadership? If you happen to have a world-class biblical scholar in your group, by all means ask him or her to lead the discussions. But in the absence of any professional Scripture scholars, or even accomplished biblical amateurs, you can still have a first-class Bible discussion. Choose two or three people to be facilitators, and have everyone read "Suggestions for Bible Discussion Groups" before beginning (page 92).

Does everyone need a guide? a Bible? Everyone in the group will need their own copy of this booklet. It contains the sections of Acts that are discussed, so a Bible is not absolutely necessary—but each participant will find it useful to have one. You should have at least one Bible on hand for your discussion. (See page 96 for recommendations.)

How do we get started? Take a look at the suggestions for Bible discussion groups (page 92) and individuals (page 95).

A History We Can Share In

Introducing the Acts of the Apostles

The philosopher George Santayana wrote that "those who cannot remember the past are condemned to repeat it." In this view, the reason for studying history is to learn about the errors that people made in the past so as to avoid committing those errors again. In remembering the past this way, a generation of Americans used the disaster of Vietnam to shape a foreign policy that shied away from foreign military involvements.

St. Luke, who wrote the history of the early Church called Acts of the Apostles, saw another purpose for remembering the past. If asked for his view, I imagine he would have said that those who are ignorant of the past cannot play their part in the present. Luke wrote his history to give his friend Theophilus a better under-standing of the origins of the gospel he had received and the Church he had joined (1:1; unless otherwise noted, all Scripture references in this booklet are to Acts). Theophilus would then be prepared to take part in the Church's life and mission.

Unlike Americans in the 1980s and 1990s who urged their fellow citizens to "learn the lessons of Vietnam" and *avoid* making the same mistakes again, Luke wanted Theophilus to learn the les-sons of the Church in Jerusalem, Joppa, Antioch, and Philippi so as to *continue* living the same life that the first Christians began to live when the Holy Spirit came to them.

Nineteen centuries later (Luke probably wrote around the year A.D. 80), Luke's history can serve the same purpose for us. Acts of the Apostles puts us in touch with the foundational events of the Church to which we belong. By understanding our history, we can enter more deeply into it. The first Christians' situation was quite different from ours, but we can share their experience, for God calls us to open ourselves to the same Spirit, to practice the same mutual love, to carry out the same mission that we read about in Luke's history. This is George Santayana in reverse: those who remember the past are enabled to repeat it.

The book that Luke wrote. If Luke could examine one of our Bibles today, he might be surprised by the location of his writ-ings. Luke composed a two-part work, but in the New Testament the parts are not placed together. Part one, Luke's Gospel, is grouped with the Gospels of Matthew, Mark, and John. Part two, Acts of the Apostles, follows the Gospels. In this arrangement, the two sections of Luke's work are separated by the Gospel of John.

While there are good reasons for this arrangement (putting all four Gospels together at the beginning of the New Testament indicates the paramount importance of Jesus himself), when reading Acts it is useful to mentally reconnect the two parts of Luke's work. Luke wrote a two-volume history because he was describing a two-stage action of God. Viewing the two volumes of the story together helps us grasp how the two stages of God's action are related to each other.

In very broad-brush terms, Luke's two-stage narrative can be summarized as follows. God had given the people of Israel a special relationship with himself and had promised that he would rescue them from oppression. He fulfilled this promise through Jesus of Nazareth, his absolutely unique Son. Through Jesus' teaching, miracles, reconciliation of sinners, and inclusion of outcasts, God made himself powerfully present to men and women. When Jesus accepted a painful death in obedience to God's plans, God raised him from death and placed him in authority over all things. That was stage one. In stage two, God sent the Holy Spirit to Jesus' followers. The Spirit enabled them to continue in the way of forgiveness, humility, and care for the needy that Jesus had initiated. And the Spirit empowered them to invite men and women everywhere to join in this graced life by believing in Jesus.

The two stages are linked by parallels. Just as God sent his Son Jesus to make his kingdom present in the world, he has now sent his Spirit to Jesus' followers, commissioning them to extend the presence of his kingdom. Just as God confirmed the authenticity of Jesus' announcement of the kingdom with powerful signs, he now gives signs to authenticate the Church's message about Jesus. Jesus had to suffer to accomplish God's purposes; suffering is likewise unavoidable for the members of the Church as they carry out their mission.

Surveying Luke's two-part narrative in this bird's-eye manner helps us identify the principal actor in the whole drama. The main character is God. God exercises the initiative. God unfolds a grand plan, first through Jesus, then through the Church. This, in turn, highlights the importance of the Church. By his Spirit, God continues through the Church the work that he began through Jesus. The Church is not an afterthought, not a mere human attempt to remember Jesus. The Church is God's instrument in the world.

I have been referring to Acts as a history. Before I proceed, it is appropriate for me to say something about the type of history it is. Acts is a history from the ancient Greco-Roman world, and ancient writers of history went about their task differently from the way that modern writers do. In Luke's culture, history writers felt freer than modern writers to reshape their material in order to bring out the meaning of past events for their readers. Scholars who have examined Luke's work closely have found many indications of the historical nature of his reports. Yet in many ways Luke has designed his narrative to convey his theology of the Spirit and of the Church. We should read Acts, then, with confidence that we are getting a fundamentally reliable picture of the early Church, but also with the awareness that Luke has not tried to present the kind of objectively factual account that would be the goal of a modern academic historian.

Acts of the Apostles is full of drama and conflict. In order to appreciate the drama, we need to see the situation of the first Christians from their point of view. Let us imagine that we could travel back to Jerusalem around the year A.D. 30. We arrive in a world that has no international Church. In fact, there are no church buildings or external signs of Christianity at all. No one keeps Sunday as a religious day; no one celebrates Christmas; no one follows a calendar counting years from the birth of Christ.

Let us suppose that we arrive in Jerusalem just after Jesus has finished appearing to his disciples following his resurrection. He has told them to remain in Jerusalem to wait for the Holy Spirit to come to them. They are now gathered in a spacious home, praying and waiting. There are only about 120 of them, men and women.

All the disciples are Jews. Quite naturally, they have a thoroughly Jewish outlook. If you were to ask them questions, they would give you Jewish answers. If you asked them who Jesus is, they would tell you that he is the Messiah—the one whom God appointed to bring liberation and holiness to the people of Israel— and that he now reigns with God. If you asked them what God is doing for Israel through Messiah Jesus, they would say that he is inaugurating the final period of history, the end times, in which he will give saving help to his people. If you looked around the room at the disciples and asked them who they are, they would identify themselves as the renewed community of Israel—the portion of Israel gathered around the Messiah.

You might ask them to explain how it is that Messiah Jesus does not seem to have a program for bringing Jews back to the land of Israel from the foreign lands where most of them live; for purifying the temple so that it might be a place where God's presence is powerfully manifested; or for freeing the Jews from the oppression of the pagan Romans. In other words, why isn't Jesus doing the things that most Jews are expecting God to accomplish for Israel? The disciples might reply that they themselves have been deeply puzzled by this, but that, while they still have questions, they have begun to grasp that Jesus is fulfilling God's plans for Israel in a different but better way.

If asked what implications the coming of the Messiah has for non-Jews, the disciples might admit that they don't know. Jewish expectations on this question varied, and Jesus did not fully clarify the matter for them. If you asked whether non-Jews without being circumcised would be able to join the renewed community of Israel founded by Jesus, the disciples might stare at you in astonishment and terminate the interview, thinking that you are no longer interested in asking serious questions.

Drama and conflict arise in Acts because God's actions transcend traditional Jewish understandings of God and Israel. God leads the disciples to bring the message of the expected-but-surprising Messiah Jesus to their fellow Jews. Some Jews accept the message and experience dramatic changes in their lives. Others reject it, and begin to argue with and persecute the disciples. Conflict occurs among the disciples also, as God leads them to a new understanding of his purposes for Gentiles.

Our reading in Week 1 is all drama. Peter, with the rest of the Twelve, makes a heartfelt appeal to his fellow Jews to reverse their thinking about Jesus and to recognize him as the promised Messiah. In a remarkable change of heart, thousands of Peter's listeners come to believe in Jesus and join Jesus' community of the renewed Israel. Among the new disciples, the salvation that Jesus brings takes concrete shape: it is not a nationalistic restoration but a life in the Spirit. A community of believers develops in which men and women experience forgiveness and joy through the Spirit as they worship God together, share a community life, and care for each other's material needs.

Before long, conflict sets in. In Week 2 the apostles' proclamation of Jesus brings them into confrontation with fellow Jews, especially the religious leaders, who do not accept Jesus because he does not fit their expectations for how God will come to save Israel.

Among the Jews of the day was an influential party called the Pharisees, who were known for being strict observers of the Mosaic law. While there was much common ground between Jesus and the Pharisees, many of them reacted against Jesus, for he claimed that God's kingdom was becoming present through himself—a claim that displaced the Mosaic law from its central role in Judaism. Jesus' followers' claim that he was now risen from the dead and ruling as Messiah and Lord over the final phase of God's dealings with Israel struck Pharisees as blasphemous. Many Pharisees hoped that their scrupulous observance of the law would hasten the day when God would grant national restoration to Israel. From their perspective, Jewish Christians' devotion to Jesus appeared to be a dangerous diversion. Our reading in Week 3 shows us a Pharisee named Saul (also called Paul), who puts himself in the forefront of efforts to excise the Christian cancer from the body of Judaism. And then—in one of the most dramatic turnarounds in the entire history of the Church—Jesus appears to Paul and convinces him that Jesus truly has both fulfilled and transcended the expectations of Judaism.

In Week 4 the focus switches to the disciples' own efforts to grasp how Jesus and the Spirit are leading them beyond traditional Jewish expectations. An extraordinary series of actions by the Spirit transports Peter across the religious and cultural divide separating Jews from Gentiles.

Despite the dramatic activity of the Spirit, the idea that Messiah Jesus wishes to be personal Lord over Gentiles is not easy for the disciples to accept. Peter's welcoming of Gentiles directly into the community of the renewed Israel without their becoming Jews clashes so fundamentally with Jewish expectations that it creates conflict within the Christian community. Thus in Week 5 we read about a council of Church leaders that gathers to discern God's will.

Once the Spirit has led the disciples to perceive that the good news about Jesus transcends its Jewish roots and reaches out to all men and women, the way is open for missionary work. In our final selection, Week 6, we observe Paul's missionary labors among Gentiles. At this point, a new source of conflict appears, as Jewish Christians preaching the one God and his Son Jesus encounter people whose beliefs and interests are based in the polytheistic culture of the time.

Questions for modern readers. Returning to the twenty-first century, we reflect on what we have learned. Like the early Jewish followers of Jesus, the Spirit leads us also into drama and conflict. God challenges us to change. For example, he challenges us to move beyond a simplistic childhood understanding of him and develop an adult understanding of his mystery—and to move beyond adolescent skepticism to a mature, trusting-despite-darkness adult faith. He wishes us to serve him in new ways, and summons us to go beyond our limited expectations of how much we might love, how self-sacrificingly we might serve, what suffering we might endure. He wishes us to experience his powerful help. He wishes to work through us to make Jesus known. He wishes us to have an impact on our world. In all these respects, reading Acts leads us to question our lives and open our hearts to a new cooperation with the Spirit of God.

THE SPIRIT ARRIVES

Questions to Begin

15 minutes
Use a question or two to get warmed up for the reading.

1   Describe your most memorable birthday. What made it special?

2   Describe a memorable dream. Did it have a message?

3   What was the most important decision you ever made on the spur of the moment? How did it turn out?

5 minutes
Read the passage aloud. Let individuals take turns reading
paragraphs.

The Reading: Acts 2:1–47

Zero Hour of the Christian World Mission

1 When the day of Pentecost had come, they were all together in one place. 2 And suddenly from heaven there came a sound like the rush of a violent wind, and it filled the entire house where they were sitting. 3 Divided tongues, as of fire, appeared among them, and a tongue rested on each of them. 4 All of them were filled with the Holy Spirit and began to speak in other languages, as the Spirit gave them ability.

5 Now there were devout Jews from every nation under heaven living in Jerusalem. 6 And at this sound the crowd gathered and was bewildered, because each one heard them speaking in the native language of each. 7 Amazed and astonished, they asked, "Are not all these who are speaking Galileans? 8 And how is it that we hear, each of us, in our own native language? . . . 11 [I]n our own languages we hear them speaking about God's deeds of power." 12 All were amazed and perplexed, saying to one another, "What does this mean?" 13 But others sneered and said, "They are filled with new wine."

14 But Peter, standing with the eleven, raised his voice and addressed them, "Men of Judea and all who live in Jerusalem, let this be known to you, and listen to what I say. 15 Indeed, these are not drunk, as you suppose, for it is only nine o'clock in the morning. 16 No, this is what was spoken through the prophet Joel:
17 'In the last days it will be, God declares,
　　that I will pour out my Spirit upon all flesh,
　　　　and your sons and your daughters shall prophesy,
　　and your young men shall see visions,
　　　　and your old men shall dream dreams.
18 Even upon my slaves, both men and women,
　　in those days I will pour out my Spirit;
　　　　and they shall prophesy.
19 And I will show portents in the heaven above
　　and signs on the earth below,
　　　　blood, and fire, and smoky mist.
20 The sun shall be turned to darkness
　　and the moon to blood,
　　　　before the coming of the Lord's great and glorious day.

21 Then everyone who calls on the name of the Lord shall be saved.'

22 "You that are Israelites, listen to what I have to say: Jesus of Nazareth, a man attested to you by God with deeds of power, wonders, and signs that God did through him among you, as you yourselves know—23 this man, handed over to you according to the definite plan and foreknowledge of God, you crucified and killed by the hands of those outside the law. 24 But God raised him up, having freed him from death, because it was impossible for him to be held in its power. . . .

32 "This Jesus God raised up, and of that all of us are witnesses. 33 Being therefore exalted at the right hand of God, and having received from the Father the promise of the Holy Spirit, he has poured out this that you both see and hear. . . . 36 Therefore let the entire house of Israel know with certainty that God has made him both Lord and Messiah, this Jesus whom you crucified."

37 Now when they heard this, they were cut to the heart and said to Peter and to the other apostles, "Brothers, what should we do?" 38 Peter said to them, "Repent, and be baptized every one of you in the name of Jesus Christ so that your sins may be forgiven; and you will receive the gift of the Holy Spirit. 39 For the promise is for you, for your children, and for all who are far away, everyone whom the Lord our God calls to him." 40 And he testified with many other arguments and exhorted them, saying, "Save yourselves from this corrupt generation." 41 So those who welcomed his message were baptized, and that day about three thousand persons were added. 42 They devoted themselves to the apostles' teaching and fellowship, to the breaking of bread and the prayers.

The Christian Community

43 Awe came upon everyone, because many wonders and signs were being done by the apostles. 44 All who believed were together and had all things in common; 45 they would sell their possessions and goods and distribute the proceeds to all, as any had need. 46 Day by day, as they spent much time together in the temple, they broke bread at home and ate their food with glad and generous hearts, 47 praising God and having the goodwill of all the people. And day by day the Lord added to their number those who were being saved.

10 minutes
Choose questions according to your interest and time.

1   Which of "God's deeds of power" were the disciples probably speaking about in verse 11? Does Peter's preaching help you answer this question?

2   What is repentance? Why does Peter call people to repent?

3   In a single sentence, how would you summarize Peter's message in verses 16–21? in verses 22–36?

4   What other responses might the crowd have made to Peter's declaration in verses 22–36? Why did they respond as they did?

5   What is the "promise" in 2:39?

6   Luke begins and ends his account of Pentecost on similar notes (compare verses 1 and 41). What might this "frame" suggest about the gift of the Spirit? In this reading, what sorts of things do people do when the Holy Spirit comes to them?

A Guide to the Reading

If participants have not read this section already, read it aloud. Otherwise go on to "Questions for Application."

2:1–3. In the large house of a prosperous Jerusalem resident, a half mile or so from the place where Jesus died and rose, 120 of his followers are praying together, seated—as Jews would sit for prayer in a synagogue. They are waiting for Jesus to fulfill a promise he made repeatedly after his resurrection (1:5, 8). It is morning.

Suddenly an explosion of mysterious wind and fire fills the house. These pyrotechnics signal an unseen event. Jesus' promise, the Holy Spirit, has arrived. Flames settle above the heads of all 120 disciples: every member of the community receives the Spirit.

The manner of the Spirit's coming evokes the moment, centuries earlier, when God made a covenant with Israel at Mount Sinai (Exodus 19–20). The sound of wind from heaven that fills the house echoes the frightening noise that announced God's presence at Sinai (Exodus 19:16; 20:22); the flames reflect God's descent to the mountain in fire (Exodus 19:18). By breathing life into the community of Jesus' followers, God is renewing his covenant with Israel.

The whole people of Israel must be invited to share in this life—a task for which the Spirit has come to empower the disciples. The flames take the shape of *tongues* because the Spirit will guide the disciples to *speak*. They receive the Spirit not just for their own benefit, but so they might serve others.

2:4–13. We may suppose that the disciples make their way to the temple, the vast courtyards of which are the only place in Jerusalem that can accommodate a large crowd. Jews from all over the world are present; some are in town for the Jewish festival of Pentecost, others are immigrants. All are astonished to hear the disciples speaking in the visitors' native languages about God's actions (2:6–11). (This marvel of communication seems different from the speaking in unknown languages that other early Christians experienced as a gift of the Spirit, since that speaking in tongues required interpretation—1 Corinthians 12, 14.)

2:14–15. Peter, as leader of the apostles, steps forward to offer an explanation. To the accusation that the disciples are drunk, he offers a laid-back response. "Drunk? Before breakfast? Give me a break!"

2:16–21. In a more serious vein, Peter explains that the disciples' unaccountably intelligible speech is evidence of God's Spirit and that the arrival of the Spirit marks the beginning of a new era in God's dealings with the human race. Peter calls it "the last days." He does not mean that the world is about to end, but that the final period of history has begun. Peter uses cosmic imagery from the prophet Joel not to predict the imminent destruction of the universe but to underline the significance of the gift of the Spirit: this is an earthshaking event!

2:22–36. Peter tells his listeners that they were mistaken about Jesus when they demanded his death seven weeks before, at the Passover festival (Luke 23:18–23). He explains that through Jesus the new age of God's dealings with the human race was dawning—as his healings and other miracles indicated (2:22). Now God has raised Jesus from death and has made him sovereign over all things, in fulfillment of a long-standing divine plan.

2:37–40. Shaken, the crowd asks Peter what they should do. "Repent!" he says. The Greek word means "change your mind." They should, of course, repent in the sense of turning away from sin; but first of all they should change their minds about Jesus, and then decide to reorient their lives toward him.

For those of Peter's listeners who had called for Jesus' death, Peter's preaching offers a precious second chance. Peter's warning not to let it slip away—"Save yourselves from this corrupt generation"—is not a blanket condemnation of the world. In Old Testament terminology, "crooked generation" referred especially to people who witnessed God's mighty acts but then walked away unaffected (Deuteronomy 1:35; 32:5; Psalm 78:8). "Don't do that!" Peter urges.

2:41–47. Thousands of men and women accept Peter's message and are baptized—the greatest miracle of Pentecost! There is ample water nearby, kept on hand for use in the temple services and for ritual bathing.

The infant Church has now come into existence. It is filled with God's Spirit and guided by the leadership group that gives it continuity with Jesus (see 1:15–26). A pattern of teaching and prayer, public testimony and mutual care quickly develops. To experience salvation through Jesus means "being added" to this community.

Questions for Application

40 minutes
Choose questions according to your interest and time.

1 Peter calls his listeners to change how they think about Jesus. How has your picture of Jesus changed over the years? What has contributed to the change? What implications has your changing picture of Jesus had for your life? What might you do to give Jesus an opportunity to reveal more of himself to you at this point in your life?

2 Where in your life is God giving you a second (or third, or tenth) chance? What difficulties, fears, or habits stand in the way of your responding to him? What do you need to do to begin to respond?

3 What does it mean to be filled with the Spirit? Who do you know that seems filled with the Spirit? How do you experience the presence of the Spirit in your life? How can Christians make themselves open to the Spirit?

4 Where in your life (family, work, parish, city) do you see signs of God's activity? How might God be calling you to cooperate with what he is doing?

5 What do you find attractive about the church in Jerusalem after Pentecost? What aspects of it offer a model for the Church today? for your parish? What is the most significant point in this reading for the Church today? Why?

6 What do verses 17 and 18 suggest about the range of people to whom God gives gifts by his Spirit? How might your attitudes toward people's sex, age, ethnic background, income, or education affect your expectations regarding their participation in the life of the Church? What could you and your parish do to encourage a greater range of people to discover and use the gifts of service that God has given them?

"Encourage each other to participate. The more people involved in a discussion, the richer it will be."

Whitney Kuniholm, *John: The Living Word,* A Fisherman Bible Study Guide

Approach to Prayer

15 minutes
Use this approach—or create your own!

✦ Pray for each other to be filled with the gifts and graces of the Holy Spirit. Let someone read Acts 2:38–39 aloud; pause for a few moments of silent reflection. Then pray together the *Come, Holy Spirit* on the next page.

The custom of praying for nine days in a row for a particular purpose (making a "novena"—from the Latin word for nine) is based on the disciples' prayer in the days between the Ascension and Pentecost, as they waited for the promised Spirit. On an individual basis you may wish to make a novena for a greater experience of the Holy Spirit by praying the *Come, Holy Spirit* for nine days in your private devotions.

A Living Tradition

Come, Holy Spirit!

This section is a supplement for individual reading.

Come, Holy Spirit. Shine
into waiting hearts and minds
      your radiance bright.
Come, you Father of the poor,
come, you giver of all store,
      come, our souls' light.
You, of comforters the best,
you, our hearts' dearest guest,
      in turmoil, kind relief;
you our respite in distress,
in the noontime, cool caress,
      comfort in our grief.
O Light making all things new,
the depths of all who hope in you
      with yourself fill.
If you should take your grace away,
nothing good in us can stay,
      all turns to ill.
Wash the grime of sin away,
irrigate our barren clay,
      our illnesses heal;
soften every hardened will,
thaw the frozen, warm the chill,
      your ways reveal.
Give to all your faithful, Lord,
to those who trust in your reward,
      all gifts of grace.
Give us virtue's blessed goal,
give a death that brings us whole
      before your face. Amen. Alleluia.

One of the most beautiful of medieval Latin hymns, this prayer may have been written by Innocent III, a thirteenth-century pope. It is sung in the liturgy of Pentecost. One scholar has remarked that it could only have been composed by someone acquainted with many sorrows but also with many encouragements from the Spirit.

Between Discussions

I was privileged to play a small supporting role when my wife Mary, after hours of disciplined breathing and some expressions of urgency and distress, pushed our first child out of the womb and into an obstetrician's waiting hands. In the aftermath of this unprecedented event, I had a leisurely opportunity to observe our son's first minutes in this world. While Mary endured some concluding unpleasantness at the hands of the obstetrician, a nurse wiped Dominic off and placed him naked in a little bed warmed by a lamp. There he was, a perfect, blue-skinned, miniature human being. I looked at his fingers and toes as though I had never seen fingers or toes before. By some incredible process, no less astonishing because of my involvement in it, a new person had made his appearance in the world, equipped with the full complement of members and organs, all properly connected and fully functioning. Tiny eyes glanced vaguely in my direction. What a kick!

I am reminded of my first meeting with Dominic when I read the second chapter of Acts. Pentecost has been called the birthday of the Church, and Luke's account does read as a description of birth—the infant Church is suddenly thrust out into the world and begins to breathe. From the first moments, the Church displays the basic elements that will grow and mature in the millennia to follow. It is remarkable how many of the Church's characteristics become visible in this single chapter of Luke's account. For instance, Luke shows us that the Church is—

1. People empowered by the Spirit. The Spirit comes to breathe life into Jesus' followers, and there is a burst of activity—marvelous signs of God's presence, inspired preaching, people turning to the Lord, strangers loving one another. We might say that the Church is the group of people among whom the Holy Spirit makes things happen.

2. A community. Each person receives the Spirit, but not as an isolated individual; the Spirit comes to a community of people joined in prayer and hope (1:13–14; 2:1). The Spirit not only enlarges the group through new members but also deepens their relationship with each other. Because they share together in the life of God, they throw their lives open to one another and use their resources to alleviate each other's needs (2:44–45).

3. A hierarchical community. Before the Spirit comes, Jesus appoints a group of twelve men as leaders (see 1:12–26; Luke 22:28–30). The leader of the leaders, Peter, makes the first public announcement of Jesus' resurrection. This leadership structure is essential for the community of those who follow Jesus (2:42). To these leaders Jesus entrusted his teaching, which is the DNA for the formation of an authentic, Christian community.

4. A community on a mission. The Spirit's coming on Pentecost is the initiating event of the day, making possible the central event, which is Peter's preaching about Jesus as Messiah and Lord. This leads to the culminating event: thousands of people come to believe in Jesus, are baptized, and join the Church. The miracle of languages, Father Joseph A. Fitzmyer, S.J., has written, conveys the idea that "the Christian message is to be borne to people of all languages and cultures."

5. A community where everyone plays a part. Peter emphasizes that the Spirit is for male and female, young and old, high class and low class (2:17–18). The Church is for everyone, from prominent male apostles to obscure impoverished widows. By contributing to the community's life of mutual love, every member contributes to the proclamation of Jesus, for the very existence of a community of love that bridges class divisions points to a divine source of power.

6. A community that worships together. Through morning and evening prayers in the temple and worship in their homes (including the Lord's Supper), the first Christians follow a pattern of celebration through which the mystery of Jesus' life, death, and resurrection continues to be present among them.

7. A community where Jesus' mother is present. Mary is among the disciples at Pentecost (see 1:14). She was already completely open to the action of God's Spirit (Luke 1:35, 38) and was the first to believe in her son. Now she is a sign of faith and hope to the disciples. In the heart of the Church, as fellow disciple and beloved mother of the Lord, she will continue to pray and bear witness to her son in every age.

Healing and Boldness

Questions to Begin

15 minutes
Use a question or two to get warmed up for the reading.

1 Describe how someone came to your help when you were in need or danger. Did you have an opportunity to express your appreciation?

2 Have you ever known someone who experienced a remarkable recovery from illness or injury after prayer, after receiving the sacrament of anointing of the sick, or after visiting a pilgrimage site such as Lourdes? If so, how did the experience affect the person who was healed? How did it affect you?

5 minutes
Read the passage aloud. Let individuals take turns reading
paragraphs.

The Reading: Acts 3:1–10; 4:5–35

A Crippled Beggar Receives More Than He Asked For

¹ One day Peter and John were going up to the temple at the hour of prayer, at three o'clock in the afternoon. ² And a man lame from birth was being carried in. People would lay him daily at the gate of the temple called the Beautiful Gate so that he could ask for alms from those entering the temple. ³ When he saw Peter and John about to go into the temple, he asked them for alms. ⁴ Peter looked intently at him, as did John, and said, "Look at us." ⁵ And he fixed his attention on them, expecting to receive something from them. ⁶ But Peter said, "I have no silver or gold, but what I have I give you; in the name of Jesus Christ of Nazareth, stand up and walk." ⁷ And he took him by the right hand and raised him up; and immediately his feet and ankles were made strong. ⁸ Jumping up, he stood and began to walk, and he entered the temple with them, walking and leaping and praising God. ⁹ All the people saw him walking and praising God, ¹⁰ and they recognized him as the one who used to sit and ask for alms at the Beautiful Gate of the temple; and they were filled with wonder and amazement at what had happened to him. . . .

Interrogation and Threats

4:5 The next day their rulers, elders, and scribes assembled in Jerusalem, ⁶ with Annas the high priest, Caiaphas, John, and Alexander, and all who were of the high-priestly family. ⁷ When they had made [them] stand in their midst, they inquired, "By what power or by what name did you do this?" ⁸ Then Peter, filled with the Holy Spirit, said to them, "Rulers of the people and elders, ⁹ if we are questioned today because of a good deed done to someone who was sick and are asked how this man has been healed, ¹⁰ let it be known to all of you, and to all the people of Israel, that this man is standing before you in good health by the name of Jesus Christ of Nazareth, whom you crucified, whom God raised from the dead. . . . ¹² There is salvation in no one else, for there is no other name under heaven given among mortals by which we must be saved."

¹³ Now when they saw the boldness of Peter and John and realized that they were uneducated and ordinary men, they were

amazed and recognized them as companions of Jesus. [14] When they saw the man who had been cured standing beside them, they had nothing to say in opposition. [15] So they ordered them to leave the council while they discussed the matter with one another. [16] They said, "What will we do with them? For it is obvious to all who live in Jerusalem that a notable sign has been done through them; we cannot deny it. [17] But to keep it from spreading further among the people, let us warn them to speak no more to anyone in this name." [18] So they called them and ordered them not to speak or teach at all in the name of Jesus. [19] But Peter and John answered them, "Whether it is right in God's sight to listen to you rather than to God, you must judge; [20] for we cannot keep from speaking about what we have seen and heard." [21] After threatening them again, they let them go, finding no way to punish them because of the people, for all of them praised God for what had happened. . . .

[23] After they were released, they went to their friends and reported what the chief priests and the elders had said to them. [24] When they heard it, they raised their voices together to God and said, "Sovereign Lord, who made the heaven and the earth, the sea, and everything in them, . . . [29] look at their threats, and grant to your servants to speak your word with all boldness, [30] while you stretch out your hand to heal, and signs and wonders are performed through the name of your holy servant Jesus." [31] When they had prayed, the place in which they were gathered together was shaken; and they were all filled with the Holy Spirit and spoke the word of God with boldness.

Caring for Needy Brothers and Sisters

[32] Now the whole group of those who believed were of one heart and soul, and no one claimed private ownership of any possessions, but everything they owned was held in common. [33] With great power the apostles gave their testimony to the resurrection of the Lord Jesus, and great grace was upon them all. [34] There was not a needy person among them, for as many as owned lands or houses sold them and brought the proceeds of what was sold. [35] They laid it at the apostles' feet, and it was distributed to each as any had need.

10 minutes
Choose questions according to your interest and time.

1 The word *name* is used frequently in this reading. Find the verses where it occurs. What does the word seem to mean in these verses? What other word might be substituted for it?

2 Peter speaks of being "saved" (4:12). Based solely on this week's and last week's readings, what effects did the first Christians in Jerusalem experience when they believed in Jesus? What were they saved from?

3 Compare the responses to Peter's preaching about Jesus in chapter 4 (4:13–18, 21) and chapter 2 (2:37). What might account for the difference?

4 What does 3:6 tell us about the effects of 2:44–45 and 4:34–35 on the leaders of the Christian community in Jerusalem?

5 What do this week's and last week's readings indicate about Peter's role in the church in Jerusalem?

A Guide to the Reading

If participants have not read this section already, read it aloud. Otherwise go on to "Questions for Application."

3:1. At the hours of the daily sacrifices—early morning and midafternoon—laypeople would join the Jewish priests in prayer in the vast temple courtyard (here called "the temple"). Thus we see Peter and John climbing the steps to the temple mount.

We might think it odd for the Christian leaders to continue participating in Jewish worship. But at this point, the members of the Christian movement see what God is doing among them simply as the fulfillment of his purposes for Israel. Jesus is the Messiah, the one whom God designated to save Israel (2:36). To an outside observer, Jesus' followers would have looked like a renewal movement within Judaism. So Peter and John feel perfectly natural about praying with their fellow Jews in the temple.

3:2–6. St. John Chrysostom, a fourth-century bishop and biblical commentator, observed that the unplanned nature of the healing suggests that Peter had no ambition to make a name for himself as a healer. St. Bede, an eighth-century English monk and scholar, pointed out that the apostles' lack of spare change showed they were not dipping into the contributions for the poor that passed through their hands (see 4:32–35).

3:7–8. Peter grasps the hand that the man continues to hold out for a coin and gives him something better. St. Ephrem suggested that the man leapt around awkwardly because he had not yet gotten the hang of walking!

3:9–4:4. The sight of the man bounding through the temple courtyard draws a large crowd. Peter makes it clear to them that *he* has not healed the man; Jesus has done it. Peter proclaims that Jesus is the Messiah and appeals to his fellow Jews to turn to Jesus. Temple officials soon show up, annoyed that Peter is preaching about Jesus' resurrection, and lock up the two apostles for the night.

4:8–12. The next morning, brought before the temple's governing council, Peter is "filled with the Holy Spirit." This does not refer to a sudden burst of holiness or a spiritual experience but to the help that God is giving him to give testimony to Jesus. In Catholic tradition this sort of divine assistance is called "actual grace"—grace to take on the action or task at hand.

Peter begins his address respectfully: "Rulers of the people and elders." But then he very boldly declares not only that the risen Jesus has healed the man; he goes on to stress the irreconcilable conflict between the religious leaders' view of Jesus and God's view of Jesus. Peter wants to make it absolutely clear that Jesus alone is God's agent for dealing with the human race (4:12; see the *Catechism of the Catholic Church,* sections 432, 839–848).

4:13. The council is astonished by Peter's boldness—but not as amazed as readers who also know about Peter's earlier cowardice (Luke 22:54–62), when he had intended to follow Jesus courageously (Luke 22:31–34) but discovered his own weakness. Now the Holy Spirit is enabling Peter to be the brave man he wanted to be then.

4:14–18. Unwilling to revise their opinion of Jesus, but unable to deny the healing, the council members resort to what scholar Luke Timothy Johnson terms "damage control." Their hostility to Jesus is evident in their reluctance even to speak his name (4:17).

4:19–30. Given the temple council's threats, the Christians might easily have decided to lay low or leave town. Only a few weeks before, the council had engineered the crucifixion of Jesus. But, as Joseph Fitzmyer points out, the Christians "do not pray to be spared persecution but beg rather for the grace of 'courageous speech'"—the kind of bold declaration of the truth that Peter just showed (4:13). Their prayer for boldness does not necessarily mean that they *feel* brave, but it does indicate a desire to *be* brave and an awareness that they need God's help.

4:32–35. Again a description of the Christian community follows a narrative about apostolic preaching (compare to 2:43–47). The Holy Spirit is working among the first Christians along inward and outward dimensions. Notice how the statement about the apostles' public testimony to Jesus is sandwiched into the description of the Christians' care for needy members (4:33). Community life and public testimony are closely related: the proclamation of Jesus draws credibility from the mutual service that outsiders can see among his followers. Some members bear witness to Jesus especially in speech, others especially in loving service; together, their witness to Jesus is both articulate and persuasive.

Questions for Application

40 minutes
Choose questions according to your interest and time.

---

1 What are your gifts and resources? Where are you tempted to use them for yourself rather than for other people? What single action, even a small one, could you take to counter this tendency?

---

2 In what ways does the Church today speak messages that are controversial—accepted by some, rejected by others? When does being a Christian today involve taking an unpopular position? What is your experience of this?

---

3 Reread 4:20 and consider your own experience of Christ. To whom do you speak about what you have seen and heard?

---

4 Where do you most need "actual grace"? Where do you most need the help of the Holy Spirit to become the person God created you to be? How could you cooperate more with the Spirit in this part of your life?

---

5 Put yourself in the place of the Christians who heard Peter and John's report (4:23). What would *you* then ask God for?

6 Reread 2:43–47 and 4:32–35. What terms might be used to describe the kind of relationship that the first Christians had with one another? If you were to view the needy members of your church community in this way, what would you do differently? Who *are* the needy members of your church community?

7 From the description of the church in Jerusalem in this week's and last week's readings, how would you have felt about joining it?

"Application is the reason for Bible study; be sure you allow plenty of time for it."

Foundations for Christian Living Series

Approach to Prayer

15 minutes
Use one of these approaches—or create your own!

✦ Pray for courage in bearing witness to Christ or in dealing with
weakness or difficulty. Begin
with an Our Father. Allow a few
minutes for silent prayer or for
participants who wish to briefly
mention an area of need. Then
pray this prayer together.

Come, Holy Spirit, fill the hearts
of your faithful; enkindle in us
the fire of your love. Send forth
your Spirit, and we shall be
created, and you shall renew the
face of the earth. O God, who by
the light of your Holy Spirit did
instruct the hearts of your faithful, grant that by that same Holy
Spirit we may be truly wise and
ever rejoice in his consolations,
through Jesus Christ our Lord.
Amen.

✦ Reread 3:8. Shout praises to
God and leap around. (Out-of-
shape discussion groups should
exercise caution.)

Saints in the Making

Wrestling with the Spirit

This section is a supplement for individual reading.

In the early 1930s a young Russian immigrant in Toronto struggled to discern God's will. Catherine de Hueck had grown up in an affluent family, but she had felt a desire to be poor. When she was in first grade, a nun in her school would take the class to a statue of St. Francis of Assisi and tell stories about his giving away his wealth. "Someday I will be just like him," the girl said to herself. "I will go and live with the poor."

Years later, Catherine lost everything in the Communist revolution and for several years lived in involuntary poverty in Canada and the United States. With intelligence and hard work, she eventually achieved a comfortable life again. But then the desire for poverty returned, along with a vague plan for becoming a Christian presence among Toronto's poorest residents.

To the priests that Catherine consulted, her idea seemed a bit crazy. But the archbishop, Neil McNeil, thought there was something to it. He advised her to take a year to pray and consider it.

Looking back four decades later, she wrote that the specific details of that year of discernment were vague in her memory. "I was wrestling with the Spirit—you might almost call me an 'early Pentecostal'! They are wrestlers with the Spirit too. . . . The Archbishop had approved my vocation, generally speaking. . . . What was not so clear was, Should I do it? Should I leave everything behind? Should I sell all I possessed? Should I, or shouldn't I? . . . When you are wrestling with the Spirit like this, the things of the world become slightly remote."

At the end of the year, Catherine was clear enough about God's purposes to take the next step. She quit her high-paying job, gave away her possessions, and began a very poor life in an immigrant section of Toronto.

In time, Catherine—better known by her later married name, Catherine Doherty—founded a community called Madonna House, in Combermere, Ontario. Madonna House continues, in Canada, the United States, and other countries, as a group of laypeople and priests committed to prayer, poverty, and service to the poor. Catherine died in 1985.

Between Discussions

If you reached the end of the reading for Week 2 wondering whether the early Christians could really have been as charitable toward each other as Luke recounts, the answer is yes and no—as Luke himself shows. On the positive side, Luke cites the example of a man named Joseph Barnabas, who sold his rural property and gave the proceeds to the apostles to give to the poor (4:36–37). On the other hand, a couple named Ananias and Sapphira who also sold some property tucked away a portion of the proceeds for themselves while pretending to present all of it to the apostles (5:1–2). Their motive is not clearly apparent, but perhaps they wanted people to think they were more generous than they were.

No community rule required members to hand over all their money (5:4); Ananias and Sapphira went wrong not in keeping their money but in lying about it. Their lie implicitly denied that God was present in any special way within the Christian community. What followed, however, revealed the powerful presence of the Spirit. Informed by the Spirit, Peter confronted the couple with their deception and, perhaps from shock and shame, they collapsed and died (5:3–11). The story records a highly unusual instance of God's judgment and does not set a pattern for God's dealings with us. But it stands as a warning against the view that God is distant from the Church or ill informed about what its members are doing.

After some healings, which testify further to the Spirit's presence in the Church (5:12–16), the apostles are again forced to appear before the temple council (5:17–42). The apostles boldly declare their commitment to speak the truth about Jesus. The council gives them a second warning—this time with a beating.

Back home with their Christian brothers and sisters, the apostles find themselves dealing with a dispute about care for the widows in the community. The Greek-speaking Jewish Christians complain that their widows are receiving less than the widows among the Aramaic-speaking Jewish Christians. The Twelve propose that the members of the community select men from among the Greek-speaking wing of the community to help remedy the problem, and seven are chosen (6:1–6).

The most common opinion is that these men were, in effect, deacons, whose commission was to administer care for the poor; Luke, however, does not portray them as functioning this way. In fact, the Seven act like the apostles, preaching and working miracles (chapters 7 and 8). Thus another possible view is that the Seven were chosen in some sense to extend the leadership of the Twelve: the Seven are to lead the Jewish Christians who are culturally Greek, while the Twelve lead those who are culturally Semitic. If this is so, the ordination of the Seven gives us insight into how the Twelve passed on their authority in an orderly way to the next generation of Christian leaders.

The ordination of leaders for the Greek-speaking Jewish Christians is an example of how the Church accommodates cultural diversity while maintaining unity in the faith (see the *Catechism of the Catholic Church,* section 814). Scholar James D. G. Dunn observes: "Diversity, in language and culture, and presumably in social composition too, was part of the first church more or less from the start. There was never a time when the Church did not know the tensions which come from diversity of culture and viewpoint and defects in organization!"

The apostles have been given two warnings to stop preaching about Jesus. In Jewish practice, after two warnings comes punishment. As it turns out, it is one of the Seven, Stephen, who suffers the penalty for outspokenness. In a lengthy speech to the temple council, Stephen reminds his listeners of God's dealings with upright men in the past—Abraham, Joseph, and Moses—and points to Jesus as *the* Upright One whom God has sent in their own day to complete God's plans for Israel. Stephen criticizes the religious leaders for presuming that they have God boxed up in the temple and thus missing his supreme representative, Jesus.

Stephen's accusation provokes a riot. He is dragged out of the city and stoned to death. His dying words are a prayer for God to forgive his attackers. Joseph Fitzmyer points out that while Stephen harshly criticizes the Jerusalem Jews for being obdurate and resisting the Holy Spirit, he nevertheless calls down God's mercy on them even as they stone him.

WHO ARE YOU, LORD?

Questions to Begin

15 minutes
Use a question or two to get warmed up for the reading.

1 What is the biggest surprise you ever had when traveling?

2 Describe a situation in which you criticized or made fun of someone (parent, teacher, boss, friend) and that person later confronted you with what you said. How did it turn out? What did you learn?

3 When have you had to overcome people's initial distrust of you in a new situation, perhaps because of your race, age, dress, accent?

5 minutes
Read the passage aloud. Let individuals take turns reading
paragraphs. (If participants have not already read "What's
Happened," read that aloud also. Otherwise skip it.)

What's Happened

Stephen, a leader among the Christians in Jerusalem, dies as the
first Christian martyr—the first follower of Jesus to lose his life
through "bearing witness" to his Lord. Among those who join in
the lynching: a man named Saul.

The Reading: Acts 8:1, 3; 9:1–30

Jesus Reveals Himself to a Persecutor

¹ That day a severe persecution began against the church in Jerusalem,
and all except the apostles were scattered throughout the countryside
of Judea and Samaria. . . . ³ Saul was ravaging the church by entering
house after house; dragging off both men and women, he committed
them to prison. . . .
     ⁹:¹ Saul, still breathing threats and murder against the dis-
ciples of the Lord, went to the high priest ² and asked him for letters
to the synagogues at Damascus, so that if he found any who belonged
to the Way, men or women, he might bring them bound to Jerusalem.
³ Now as he was going along and approaching Damascus, suddenly a
light from heaven flashed around him. ⁴ He fell to the ground and
heard a voice saying to him, "Saul, Saul, why do you persecute me?"
⁵ He asked, "Who are you, Lord?" The reply came, "I am Jesus, whom
you are persecuting. ⁶ But get up and enter the city, and you will be
told what you are to do." ⁷ The men who were traveling with him
stood speechless because they heard the voice but saw no one. ⁸ Saul
got up from the ground, and though his eyes were open, he could see
nothing; so they led him by the hand and brought him into Damascus. ⁹ For three days he was without sight, and neither ate nor drank.

A Conversion That No One Expected

¹⁰ Now there was a disciple in Damascus named Ananias. The Lord
said to him in a vision, "Ananias." He answered, "Here I am, Lord."
¹¹ The Lord said to him, "Get up and go to the street called Straight,
and at the house of Judas look for a man of Tarsus named Saul. At
this moment he is praying, ¹² and he has seen in a vision a man named

Ananias come in and lay his hands on him so that he might regain his sight." 13 But Ananias answered, "Lord, I have heard from many about this man, how much evil he has done to your saints in Jerusalem; 14 and here he has authority from the chief priests to bind all who invoke your name." 15 But the Lord said to him, "Go, for he is an instrument whom I have chosen to bring my name before Gentiles and kings and before the people of Israel; 16 I myself will show him how much he must suffer for the sake of my name." 17 So Ananias went and entered the house. He laid his hands on Saul and said, "Brother Saul, the Lord Jesus, who appeared to you on your way here, has sent me so that you may regain your sight and be filled with the Holy Spirit." 18 And immediately something like scales fell from his eyes, and his sight was restored. Then he got up and was baptized, 19 and after taking some food, he regained his strength.

For several days he was with the disciples in Damascus, 20 and immediately he began to proclaim Jesus in the synagogues, saying, "He is the Son of God." 21 All who heard him were amazed and said, "Is not this the man who made havoc in Jerusalem among those who invoked this name? And has he not come here for the purpose of bringing them bound before the chief priests?" 22 Saul became increasingly more powerful and confounded the Jews who lived in Damascus by proving that Jesus was the Messiah.

23 After some time had passed, the Jews plotted to kill him, 24 but their plot became known to Saul. They were watching the gates day and night so that they might kill him; 25 but his disciples took him by night and let him down through an opening in the wall, lowering him in a basket.

26 When he had come to Jerusalem, he attempted to join the disciples; and they were all afraid of him, for they did not believe that he was a disciple. 27 But Barnabas took him, brought him to the apostles, and described for them how on the road he had seen the Lord, who had spoken to him, and how in Damascus he had spoken boldly in the name of Jesus. 28 So he went in and out among them in Jerusalem, speaking boldly in the name of the Lord. 29 He spoke and argued with the Hellenists; but they were attempting to kill him. 30 When the believers learned of it, they brought him down to Caesarea and sent him off to Tarsus.

10 minutes
Choose questions according to your interest and time.

1 Why does Jesus say to Paul, "Why do you persecute *me*?" rather than "Why do you persecute *my followers*?" (9:4; italics mine)? What does Jesus' choice of words imply about his relationship with his followers?

2 What do you suppose Paul did or thought during his days of blindness before Ananias came to him? What purpose might this period have served for Paul?

3 Why didn't God restore Paul's sight directly rather than through Ananias?

4 Judging just from this reading, in what ways did Paul's conversion change him? In what ways did he remain the same person?

5 In portrayals of Paul's conversion, artists usually depict him being knocked off his horse when Jesus appears to him. What's wrong with this picture?

A Guide to the Reading

If participants have not read this section already, read it aloud. Otherwise go on to "Questions for Application."

8:1–3. If Luke had recorded the stoning of Stephen with a camcorder rather than a pen, I imagine he would have panned through the crowd until his camera came to rest on a face distorted with rage—the face of Saul of Tarsus (7:60–8:1). Saul is the first known organizer of an anti-Christian persecution. After Stephen's death, Saul leads a concerted effort to destroy the Christian community. Of Saul in 8:3, Luke Timothy Johnson writes: "Everything in the description points to arbitrary and violent anger."

Like many other Pharisees, Saul probably reacted with hostility to Jesus because Jesus rejected the Pharisees' concept of Israel as a community that would strictly observe their interpretations of the Mosaic law in the hope that God would bring national vindication. Saul was his Semitic name. He is better known by his Greco-Roman name, Paul (for simplicity, we will refer to him hereafter as Paul).

9:1–7. Paul attempts to extend the persecution to Damascus, a Syrian city 135 miles north of Jerusalem. As he nears Damascus, a light flashes around him and a voice cries out his name. When Paul questions his identity, the speaker makes a terrifying response: "I am Jesus." The man whom Paul thought was dead is alive! And he is well aware of Paul's hostility to him: "Why do you persecute me?" Yet Jesus has not revealed himself in order to crush Paul but to induce him to change his mind. Jesus has work in mind for this persecutor of his followers.

9:8–9. Paul gets up from the ground blinded—his blindness is not a punishment but a sign of his helplessness before the power of the one he had been opposing. Scholar F. F. Bruce argues that Paul's abstinence from food and drink is not so much an expression of his seeking God as a sign that his encounter with Jesus has shaken him to the depths of his being.

9:10–16. Ananias offers God some information about Paul (hasn't God heard why Paul was coming to Damascus?). God does not seem annoyed by Ananias's objection, but enters into a real conversation with his servant (similarly 10:9–16). But in the end, God does insist on being obeyed.

9:17–19. Joseph Fitzmyer points out that Ananias would have been among those whom Paul planned to cart off to prison in Jerusalem. It must have been humbling for Paul to realize that the Lord was using one of Paul's intended victims to receive him into the Christian community.

A special revelation brought Paul to recognize Jesus and repudiate persecution of his followers. But now Paul receives the Spirit and becomes a member of the Church through the means that is common to everyone—baptism. No matter how directly God may reveal himself to a person, conversion to Jesus is completed only by becoming a member of his body.

Paul's conversion is unusually dramatic, yet it involves aspects of God's dealings that many other people have experienced. Paul did not seek Jesus; Jesus sought Paul. Paul learned that Jesus had been present with him even when Paul did not yet know him, even when Paul rejected him. God dealt with Paul according to Paul's particular needs and personality: a violent persecutor was given an almost violent confrontation with the truth that left him temporarily helpless and receptive to the Spirit. God showed Paul that he had a plan for his life—a plan that Paul could discover only by recognizing his own blindness, by coming to grips with who Jesus is, and by deciding to follow him.

9:20–25. It was unprecedented in biblical history for God to call into his service someone who had persecuted his people. Thus God's calling and commissioning of Paul strikingly displays the divine mercy. Paul's life will now bear witness to a God who summons sinners great and small—not only to forgiveness and reconciliation with himself but also to play a role in advancing his kingdom of forgiveness and reconciliation (1 Timothy 1:12–17).

9:26–30. Paul's visit to Jerusalem—the center of opposition to the Christian movement—illustrates his continuing boldness. And, since the apostles are in Jerusalem, Paul's interest in visiting the city also shows his interest in keeping in touch with the "mother church." The unity that the Spirit began to give the Church on Pentecost continues to be embodied in new ways as the Christian movement spreads out and grows in numbers.

Questions for Application

40 minutes
Choose questions according to your interest and time.

1 Why does God sometimes use periods of darkness to bring a person into a different and better period of life? How have you experienced this process? What effect should this experience have on your life today?

2 How might you be affected by the realization that God has specifically chosen you to play some part in his purposes in the world? Have you ever had this realization?

3 Drawing on your own experience and that of people you know, as well as on the story of Paul, what does conversion to Christ mean? In what ways can a person who already believes in God experience conversion?

4 What people in your life have played the role of Ananias, welcoming you into the life of the Church and praying for you? What can you learn from these people? How can you imitate them?

5 Paul immediately began to share the knowledge of Jesus he had received. How can you share with others something of the spiritual and material resources God has given you?

6 When have you been slow to believe that someone has changed for the better? Have you ever been on the receiving end of such negative expectations? How do negative expectations like this affect people?

"Without prayer, Bible study can dissolve into just another intellectual exercise."

Jerome Kodell, O.S.B., *The Catholic Bible Study Handbook*

Approach to Prayer

15 minutes
Use this approach—or create your own!

✦ Pray for men and women to hear God's call to conversion, especially those who seem to be in special need of God's grace and help. Ask someone in the group to reread Acts 9:1–6. Take a few minutes for participants, if they wish, simply to name those they wish to pray for. Then pray together this prayer to St. Paul.

St. Paul, once a persecutor of the Church and then an apostle of Christ, God shone his light on you to show you that you were traveling on the wrong road. He treated you mercifully when you were behaving as his enemy. By your preaching, you brought the good news of God's forgiveness and grace to many people. Now by your prayers may God's kindness and truth come to these for whom we pray, for the glory of God. Amen.

A Living Tradition

Humbled by God

This section is a supplement for individual reading.

The earliest known Christian teacher to write about Acts was St. Ephrem the Syrian, a deacon who lived in Nisibis, in modern southeast Turkey, in the fourth century. Here are some of his thoughts on Paul's dramatic conversion.

Saul was more violently opposed to the Church than even the priests were. On his own initiative he went and obtained a decree from them against the Christians and set out to persecute them. But out of consideration for the Church, God made Saul a disciple before he could carry out all the persecution he strove to accomplish.

God blinded Saul with light and terrified him. Saul fell to the ground. Before the voice spoke, he lay there stunned, wondering who had struck him from heaven—not having any idea that it was Jesus, because he did not think Jesus was risen from the dead. When a voice asked him, "Saul, why do you persecute me?" Saul was thrown into confusion. He thought to himself, *I am persecuting on behalf of heaven. How can I be persecuting him who dwells in heaven?* So Saul said, "Who are you, my Lord, who endure persecution in heaven? I persecute Jesus, who is among the dead, with his disciples." Then the Lord said to him, "I *am* Jesus, whom you are persecuting!"

Saul was terror-stricken by this. He was very much afraid that he might not ever get up from the earth where he was thrown, that he might never see the light of day again. His teeth were chattering with fear at the thought of punishment too great to bear. So he asked, "Lord, what do you want me to do? For whatever I have done up until now, I did in ignorance. Let me become your preacher, so that I might make amends for my persecution."

Nevertheless, God did not heal him on the spot, but had him come into Damascus blinded, so that all in the city might come and see him, and take warning from the sign that was imposed on him. Taking him by the hands, his companions led him into Damascus, to which he had set out with such great arrogance. The man who had come to the city to bind up and draw out others was himself drawn into the city like one bound up.

Between Discussions

P aul, who has returned home for a spell (9:28–30), will soon reemerge to become the great evangelizer of the Gentiles. But he will not be the first to penetrate the religious and cultural barrier between Jews and Gentiles. The Christian mission's breakthrough into the non-Jewish world will come through Peter, as we will read next week (chapter 10). Consequently, all the missionary work that follows, throughout the world and down the millennia, will stem from the pioneer witness-bearing of Peter, the leader of the apostles. As the Church grows and spreads, it remains in continuity with its beginnings in Jesus' chosen group of apostles, who were witnesses of his life, death, and resurrection.

In preparation for the breakthrough event, Luke turns his attention once more to Peter. Peter leaves Jerusalem to make a pastoral visitation to Jewish-Christian communities that may have been founded by Philip, one of the Seven (8:40). In the town of Lydda, Peter heals a man named Aeneas who has been bedridden for eight years. In the nearby town of Joppa, he raises from death a woman named Tabitha, or Dorcas (9:32–43). It is a notable pattern both in Luke's Gospel and in Acts that he often reports miracles in pairs of narratives, one dealing with a man, the other with a woman. As Ben Witherington observes: "This deliberate pattern is Luke's way of suggesting that the good news and all the aspects of salvation . . . are intended equally for men and women."

These two miracles cap a series of wonders and signs worked by Peter (3:1–6; 5:14–16). Further miracles will follow in the ministry of Paul (14:8–10; 20:7–12). Miraculous healings and restorations of life were undeniably prominent in the ministry of the first leaders of the Church. Such extraordinary phenomena naturally attracted attention and gave Christians an opening to talk about Jesus. But the miracles were more than attention getters, more even than expressions of God's love for the few individuals who directly benefited. Jesus worked healings as a sign that God's kingdom was becoming present in the world through him (Luke 11:20). The continuation of the same miraculous signs through his followers demonstrates that Jesus' death and resurrection has now inaugurated the final age in God's relationship with men and women. It was to confirm this message, Luke reports, that Christians in the church in Jerusalem asked God to heal people through the ministry of the apostles (4:24–30).

The early Christians welcomed healings as a way of helping other people recognize God's mercy through Jesus. But they did not expect that these powerful signs of God's presence would make their own lives easy. Healings did not make Peter and Paul wealthy. And while they undoubtedly gave Peter and Paul a certain notoriety, the healings also often embroiled them in dangerous disputes with political and religious authorities (chapters 3–4). Thus the Christians prayed not only for miracles but also for courage to speak boldly and accept their share of suffering—a courage which for many of them may itself have seemed miraculous!

We might take note of both expectations. The early Christians expected that God would display his mercy to people in extraordinary ways. And they expected that they themselves would encounter hardships in the course of making Jesus known. How do their expectations compare with our own? Are we as open as they were to the Spirit's acting in powerful and unpredictable ways? Do we pray for the courage to face difficulties in Christ's service? Personally, I prefer safe routines and zero suffering. But reading Acts reminds me that God has greater and nobler expectations for my life.

After the incidents with Aeneas and Tabitha, Peter stays on in the home of a tanner in Joppa, on the Mediterranean coast, in the vicinity of modern Tel Aviv. He has reached the edge of Jewish settlement in Palestine; north of Joppa the towns along the coast are mostly gentile. There is a kind of theological geography in Luke's account. Peter has come to a religious and cultural borderland. The gospel has spread up to that border; will it now cross over into the gentile world?

Peter would have been very reluctant to carry the gospel across the boundary. The Jewish consciousness of having been chosen by God and called to a special way of life erected a barrier between Jews and the rest of the world. Left to himself, Peter probably would have continued to bring the announcement of the Jewish Messiah only to fellow Jews. But Peter was not going to be left to himself.

The Spirit Leads the Way

Questions to Begin

15 minutes
Use a question or two to get warmed up for the reading.

---

1 When have you walked into a situation and met with a big surprise?

---

2 How do you react when someone interrupts you while you are speaking?
❑ I keep right on talking.
❑ I meekly give way.
❑ I let the other person speak, but show my annoyance.
❑ I feel annoyed, but try not to show it.
❑ I listen to the other person, but try to complete my thought.

5 minutes
Read the passage aloud. Let individuals take turns reading
paragraphs.

The Reading: Acts 10:1–48

Complementary Visions

[1] In Caesarea there was a man named Cornelius, a centurion of the Italian Cohort, as it was called. [2] He was a devout man who feared God with all his household; he gave alms generously to the people and prayed constantly to God. [3] One afternoon at about three o'clock he had a vision in which he clearly saw an angel of God coming in and saying to him, "Cornelius." [4] He stared at him in terror and said, "What is it, Lord?" He answered, "Your prayers and your alms have ascended as a memorial before God. [5] Now send men to Joppa for a certain Simon who is called Peter. . . . " [7] When the angel who spoke to him had left, he called two of his slaves and a devout soldier from the ranks of those who served him, [8] and after telling them everything, he sent them to Joppa.

[9] About noon the next day, as they were on their journey and approaching the city, Peter went up on the roof to pray. [10] He became hungry and wanted something to eat; and while it was being prepared, he fell into a trance. [11] He saw the heaven opened and something like a large sheet coming down, being lowered to the ground by its four corners. [12] In it were all kinds of four-footed creatures and reptiles and birds of the air. [13] Then he heard a voice saying, "Get up, Peter; kill and eat." [14] But Peter said, "By no means, Lord; for I have never eaten anything that is profane or unclean." [15] The voice said to him again, a second time, "What God has made clean, you must not call profane." [16] This happened three times, and the thing was suddenly taken up to heaven.

[17] Now while Peter was greatly puzzled about what to make of the vision that he had seen, suddenly the men sent by Cornelius appeared. They . . . were standing by the gate. . . . [23] So Peter invited them in and gave them lodging.

The next day he got up and went with them, and some of the believers from Joppa accompanied him. [24] The following day they came to Caesarea. Cornelius was expecting them and had called together his relatives and close friends. [25] On Peter's arrival Cornelius met him, . . . [27] [a]nd as he talked with him, he went in and found that many had assembled; [28] and he said to them, "You yourselves know that it is unlawful for a Jew to associate with or to visit a Gentile; but God has shown me that I should not call anyone profane or unclean. ²⁹ So when I was sent for, I came without objection. Now may I ask why you sent for me?"

³⁰ Cornelius replied, "Four days ago at this very hour, at three o'clock, I was praying in my house when suddenly a man in dazzling clothes stood before me. ³¹ He said, 'Cornelius, your prayer has been heard and your alms have been remembered before God. ³² Send therefore to Joppa and ask for Simon, who is called Peter. . . .' ³³ Therefore I sent for you immediately, and you have been kind enough to come. So now all of us are here in the presence of God to listen to all that the Lord has commanded you to say."

The Gentile Pentecost

³⁴ Then Peter began to speak to them: "I truly understand that God shows no partiality, ³⁵ but in every nation anyone who fears him and does what is right is acceptable to him. ³⁶ You know the message he sent to the people of Israel, preaching peace by Jesus Christ. . . . ³⁸ how God anointed Jesus of Nazareth with the Holy Spirit and with power; how he went about doing good and healing all who were oppressed by the devil, for God was with him. ³⁹ We are witnesses to all that he did both in Judea and in Jerusalem. They put him to death by hanging him on a tree; ⁴⁰ but God raised him on the third day and allowed him to appear, ⁴¹ not to all the people but to us who were chosen by God as witnesses, and who ate and drank with him after he rose from the dead. ⁴² He commanded us to preach to the people and to testify that he is the one ordained by God as judge of the living and the dead. ⁴³ All the prophets testify about him that everyone who believes in him receives forgiveness of sins through his name."

⁴⁴ While Peter was still speaking, the Holy Spirit fell upon all who heard the word. ⁴⁵ The circumcised believers who had come with Peter were astounded that the gift of the Holy Spirit had been poured out even on the Gentiles, ⁴⁶ for they heard them speaking in tongues and extolling God. Then Peter said, ⁴⁷ "Can anyone withhold the water for baptizing these people who have received the Holy Spirit just as we have?" ⁴⁸ So he ordered them to be baptized in the name of Jesus Christ. Then they invited him to stay for several days.

Questions for Careful Reading

10 minutes
Choose questions according to your interest and time.

1 Who takes the initiative in this episode?

2 What picture of Cornelius do you get from what he says and does, as well as from what is said about him? What characters in the Gospels or in other books of the Bible might he be compared to?

3 Would you say that Peter is a good learner? Why?

4 If God was going to speak to Cornelius and Peter so directly and clearly, why didn't he give either of them the full picture of his intentions?

5 What is the climax of the episode? What makes this climax so important?

A Guide to the Reading

If participants have not read this section already, read it aloud.
Otherwise go on to "Questions for Application."

10:1–8. Cornelius is a noncommissioned officer in the Roman army. His unit, the Italian Cohort, is known to have been an auxiliary contingent of archers. That he is "a devout man who feared God" means that he is a Gentile who worships the God of Israel and leads an upright life but has not gone so far as to join the Jewish people by being circumcised. Not being Jewish, he cannot offer sacrifice in the temple. But, an angel tells him, God in effect finds his prayers and generosity to the poor as pleasing as a Jew's sacrifice (10:4).

10:9–17. Peter goes up to pray on the flat roof of the house, perhaps the only escape from a noisy household. He is confronted with a vision of food and what may be the most difficult issue he has ever had to deal with.

By requiring Jews to be different from other people, the Mosaic food regulations clearly identify Jews as a people in a special relationship with God. Erasing the food laws would blur the distinction between Jew and Gentile—an almost unthinkable possibility for a devout first-century Jew. Jews had died rather than violate the dietary laws (2 Maccabees 7). At this point in Acts, the Christians are Jews and assume that God has left standing the barrier between Israel and other peoples: the blessings of Messiah Jesus are for Israel—and for Gentiles only if they attach themselves to Israel. But the voice in the vision announces to Peter that God has stopped making a distinction between clean and unclean animals. How can that be? Peter wonders. As James D. G. Dunn writes, Peter "was faced with one of the most radical rethinks of religious principle imaginable." Joseph Fitzmyer translates Peter's response to the command to eat ritually impure animals: "Not on your life, sir!"

As earlier in the Gospel accounts, Peter is still struggling to understand what his Lord is about (Mark 8:31–33; John 13:6–10; 18:10–11).

10:23–33. God has given Cornelius and Peter complementary visions. He speaks to the two men individually not to make them independent but precisely in order to bring them together. To each, God speaks only part of his message. The two men have to put their two pieces of the puzzle together in order to see the whole picture of what God is about. Bede suggests that God's approach fosters humility.

From Peter's retelling of his vision to Cornelius (10:27–29), we can see that Peter has grasped its significance. As Dunn writes, Peter realizes that "if no animal was by nature unclean, then neither could any human being as such be so designated. Peter was now free to deal with Cornelius as he would have dealt with any fellow Jew." Peter can enter as a guest into Cornelius's house.

Cornelius's explanation brings Peter to the next stage of insight. Peter learns that God finds Cornelius acceptable. Not only has God removed the barrier between Jews and Gentiles, he has prepared the Gentiles for the good news about Jesus. Peter can now offer the gospel to Cornelius as he had been offering it to Jews in Jerusalem.

Concerning Peter and Cornelius's conversation, Luke Timothy Johnson remarks: "Each retelling . . . tells something more, as though the characters themselves grew to understand better what they were up to as they spoke to each other about it."

10:34–43. To Cornelius, his family, friends, and military and business associates, Peter presents the gospel in outline. Ben Witherington writes of 10:36, "The alert listener would hear echoes of . . . the angel's message to the unclean shepherds in Luke 2:10–14." Cornelius and company are the men and women of goodwill to whom God's peace is about to come.

10:44–48. Cornelius and his household believe Peter's message about Jesus, and the Spirit comes to them, inspiring them to burst out in praises of God, as the first disciples had done at Pentecost. Since God has obviously accepted these Gentiles as believers in his Son, Peter feels he has no choice but to acknowledge them as brothers and sisters in Christ and receive them into the Church through baptism. F. F. Bruce writes: "As at Pentecost Peter, so to speak, had used the keys of the kingdom to admit Jewish believers to the new fellowship, so now he used them to open a door of faith to Gentiles." Cornelius and his household are baptized without circumcision—without becoming Jews.

The gospel has leapt the barrier and is loose in the world.

Questions for Application

40 minutes
Choose questions according to your interest and time.

1   What have been some milestones in your own process of learning to follow the Lord?

2   When has God had to work at overcoming your resistance to his will in some area of your life?

3   What gifts for serving others has God given you? How is he calling you to fit your efforts together with those of others in the Church in order to accomplish his purposes?

4   How can a person strike a balance between holding on to what is good and true and being open to change? As people grow older, how can they remain open to learning about God and responding to him in new ways?

5 What opportunities to discuss your faith with other Christians have been most helpful to you in deepening your faith? What can you do to take more advantage of such an opportunity in your life today?

6 What might you and your parish do to be more welcoming to a wider variety of people? How could you more actively express interest in newcomers and guests and draw them in? Where might God be calling you to reach out to someone with whom you would ordinarily not have much contact?

"Any questions that come up that cannot be answered satisfactorily should be researched by the leader or a volunteer and dealt with in the next meeting if possible."

Rena Duff, *Sharing God's Word Today*

Approach to Prayer

15 minutes
Use this approach—or create your own!

✦ Express your willingness to be
surprised by God by praying
together this prayer of Cardinal
Léon Joseph Suenens.

Lord, give us the
breath of life
so that we will not
run out of breath
along the way,
so that our lungs
may always be filled
with bracing air
to help us advance
towards tomorrow
without looking back
or counting the cost . . .
Breath to hope anew,
As if life were
beginning this very
morning,
to hope against wind
and tides
because of your
presence and your
promise . . .
Your breath . . .
the Spirit who blows
where he will,
in gusts
or bursts of wind
or with that
light touch
by which you invite
us to follow
your inspirations.

Saints in the Making

The Spirit Speaks a Disturbing Word

This section is a supplement for individual reading.

In 1982 Daniel Heffernan was a middle-aged physician who had been serious about his Christian faith for many years. Besides being dedicated to his patients, Dan was a loving husband and father and was deeply involved in various renewal activities in the Church. That year, he went on a weekend retreat with a few friends.

Driving home from the retreat, Dan reflected on the great blessings that God had given him. His life was well ordered and full. But then an inner voice broke into his thoughts. "You have become complacent," the voice said.

Dan felt that this was a word from the Holy Spirit. The message was disturbing, but then, Dan thought, perhaps God wanted to disturb him for good reason. Spurred to examine his life, Dan asked himself whether God might be placing before him some new opportunity to serve. After some consideration, he realized that he had the capacity to provide medical care for at least a few of the people in his area whose medical needs were not being met by the existing health-care institutions. With help from his wife, Bev, and a few other medical professionals, Dan decided to begin a free clinic at a nearby school for people who could not afford to pay for medical attention.

Over the years since then, other physicians and medical personnel have joined Dan Heffernan. Their organization, Hope Medical Clinic, in Ypsilanti, Michigan, is a nonprofit, interdenominational Christian medical and social service organization that each year treats fifteen hundred patients who do not have medical coverage. More than forty physicians, nurse practitioners, and registered nurses volunteer their time, and a network of other physicians volunteer to take specialty referrals from the clinic. Hope Clinic has grown to include a dental clinic, food and residential programs, a jail ministry, and other forms of service, all of which are provided free of charge. After almost two decades, Dan continues to serve as the medical director.

The Spirit's post-retreat word to Dan has certainly proven to be fruitful.

Between Discussions

Most readers probably do not pay much attention to the end of Luke's account of Peter's meeting with Cornelius: "Then they invited him to stay for several days" (10:48). What could be significant about that? It seems natural that the newly baptized Cornelius would want his new Christian teacher, who had known Jesus personally, to stay around for a few follow-up questions. Out of pastoral concern, Peter would presumably be glad to do so. But, in fact, a house visit was far from natural under the circumstances. And it is Peter's being a guest of Cornelius, not his having baptized him, that becomes a point of reproach when Peter gets back to Jerusalem.

Remember Peter's own words: "It is unlawful for a Jew to associate with or to visit a Gentile" (10:28). The way most Jews interpreted the Mosaic law, Gentiles' homes were considered ritually impure, and certainly the food they served was not kosher. Thus when Peter returns to Jerusalem, some in the church criticize him: "Why did you go to uncircumcised men and eat with them?" (11:3).

In defense of his actions, Peter describes the series of events, beginning with his vision of pure and impure animals and ending with the "second Pentecost" at Cornelius's house (11:4–17). (The repetition of the story is one of Luke's ways of indicating its importance.) Peter succeeds in bringing the Jerusalem Christians to recognize that God has decided to invite non-Jews as well as Jews to faith in Jesus.

The Jerusalem Christians grant that Peter has been following the Spirit's initiative, but they now have to think through the implications of what God is doing. Through baptism, Gentiles are both joined to Christ and incorporated into his body, the Church. As members of the Church, Christians are brothers and sisters in Christ; they share meals in each other's homes and care for each other's material needs (2:46). By accepting Cornelius's hospitality, Peter began to relate to the gentile believers in just this way, as brothers and sisters in Christ. How can Jewish Christians, who follow the Mosaic law, have such a close relationship with gentile Christians, whose non-Jewish lifestyle makes them ritually impure?

In the thinking of some Jewish Christians in Peter's day, there is an obvious way to resolve the dilemma of how to be faithful Jews while being open to what God is doing with the Gentiles. In the view of these Jewish Christians, gentile Christians should complete their conversion to the Jewish Messiah by becoming Jews. The men should be circumcised; men and women should undertake to follow the Mosaic law. Then the Gentiles' salvation would be complete and Jewish believers would be able to share their community life with them. Other Jewish Christians, however, vigorously resist this apparently neat solution.

The conflict will come to a head in our next reading. The events that will precipitate the crisis are underway even as Peter speaks in Jerusalem. Jewish Christians, many of them Greek-speaking, have traveled from Jerusalem to Antioch (one of the largest cities of the Roman Empire, in present-day south-central Turkey). There they are evangelizing Greek-speaking Gentiles with remarkable results. "The hand of the Lord was with them, and a great number became believers and turned to the Lord" (11:21). Antioch becomes Cornelius's house on a grand scale.

The Jerusalem Christians welcome the influx of Gentiles in Antioch, even though their presence magnifies the theological and pastoral dilemma. The Christians are trying to follow the Spirit's initiative, even when they do not entirely understand where he is leading them. The Jerusalem church sends Barnabas as its representative to Antioch. Pleased, and apparently overwhelmed by the number of new Christians there, Barnabas goes to look for Paul and brings him to Antioch to share in the leadership.

After relating additional events (chapter 12—the murder of the apostle James, further persecution of Peter, the death of Herod Agrippa), Luke recounts how the Antioch church sends Barnabas and Paul out to evangelize on the island of Cyprus and in the region that is now central Turkey (chapters 13–14). Large numbers of Gentiles pour into the Church. The brewing crisis boils over.

Week 5

TRYING TO GRASP WHAT GOD IS DOING

Questions to Begin

15 minutes
Use a question or two to get warmed up for the reading.

1 Recall a time when you took counsel with friends or family about an important issue. What was the issue? How helpful was the consultation?

2 What is your approach to disagreements?
❏ I close my eyes and hope they go away.
❏ I assume that I must be wrong.
❏ I always try to avoid confrontation.
❏ I negotiate, compromise, and try to reach a rational conclusion.
❏ I don't address the issue directly, but make little cutting remarks to let people know where I stand.
❏ I don't put up a fight, but then play the martyr.
❏ I manipulate situations behind the scenes.
❏ I concentrate on winning at all costs.
❏ I find that sometimes a good fight clears the air.

5 minutes
*Read the passage aloud. Let individuals take turns reading
paragraphs. (If participants have not already read "What's
Happened," read that aloud also. Otherwise skip it.)*

What's Happened

Now that Peter has brought the gospel to non-Jews, other Christians do the same, on a larger scale. The church in Antioch proves
to be very mission-minded. The Christians there send Barnabas and
Paul to spread the word about Jesus to both Jews and Gentiles in
present-day Cyprus and central Turkey. Like Cornelius, the Gentiles
join the Church without becoming Jews. But once the Gentiles
are baptized, should they begin following the Mosaic law? On this
question there are sharply different views.

The Reading: Acts 15:1–35

Must Gentile Believers Become Jews?

1 Then certain individuals came down from Judea and were teaching
the brothers, "Unless you are circumcised according to the custom of
Moses, you cannot be saved." 2 And after Paul and Barnabas had no
small dissension and debate with them, Paul and Barnabas and some
of the others were appointed to go up to Jerusalem to discuss this
question with the apostles and the elders. 3 So they were sent on their
way by the church, and as they passed through both Phoenicia and
Samaria, they reported the conversion of the Gentiles, and brought
great joy to all the believers. 4 When they came to Jerusalem, they
were welcomed by the church and the apostles and the elders, and
they reported all that God had done with them. 5 But some believers
who belonged to the sect of the Pharisees stood up and said, "It is
necessary for them to be circumcised and ordered to keep the law
of Moses."

   6 The apostles and the elders met together to consider this
matter. 7 After there had been much debate, Peter stood up and said
to them, "My brothers, you know that in the early days God made a
choice among you, that I should be the one through whom the Gentiles would hear the message of the good news and become believers.
8 And God, who knows the human heart, testified to them by giving
them the Holy Spirit, just as he did to us; 9 and in cleansing their
hearts by faith he has made no distinction between them and us.

10 Now therefore why are you putting God to the test by placing on the neck of the disciples a yoke that neither our ancestors nor we have been able to bear? 11 On the contrary, we believe that we will be saved through the grace of the Lord Jesus, just as they will."

12 The whole assembly kept silence, and listened to Barnabas and Paul as they told of all the signs and wonders that God had done through them among the Gentiles. 13 After they finished speaking, James replied, "My brothers, listen to me. 14 Simeon has related how God first looked favorably on the Gentiles, to take from among them a people for his name. 15 This agrees with the words of the prophets, as it is written,

> 16 'After this I will return,
> and I will rebuild the dwelling of David, which has fallen;
>> from its ruins I will rebuild it,
>> and I will set it up,
> 17 so that all other peoples may seek the Lord—
>> even all the Gentiles over whom my name has been
>> called.
>> Thus says the Lord, who has been making these
>> things 18 known from long ago.'

19 Therefore I have reached the decision that we should not trouble those Gentiles who are turning to God, 20 but we should write to them to abstain only from things polluted by idols and from fornication and from whatever has been strangled and from blood. . . . "

22 Then the apostles and the elders, with the consent of the whole church, decided to choose men from among their members and to send them to Antioch with Paul and Barnabas. They sent Judas called Barsabbas, and Silas, leaders among the brothers, 23 with the . . . letter. . . .

30 So they were sent off and went down to Antioch. When they gathered the congregation together, they delivered the letter. 31 When its members read it, they rejoiced at the exhortation. 32 Judas and Silas, who were themselves prophets, said much to encourage and strengthen the believers. 33 After they had been there for some time, they were sent off in peace by the believers to those who had sent them. 35 But Paul and Barnabas remained in Antioch, and there, with many others, they taught and proclaimed the word of the Lord.

10 minutes
Choose questions according to your interest and time.

1 Why would the Christians in Antioch send representatives to the church in Jerusalem to resolve the issue that had arisen (15:1–2)?

2 What picture does this reading paint of the relationships between Christians in different localities in the early years of the Church?

3 On what kinds of evidence and what sorts of arguments do the apostles and elders base their decision?

4 How would you describe the personal relationships among the main figures in this reading? Cite particular verses to support your view. How does the kind of relationship they have with each other affect their ability to deal with disagreement?

5 What are the elements of the process that these early Christians follow for resolving their disagreement? What lessons could be drawn from this for how disagreements should be handled in the Church today?

A Guide to the Reading

If participants have not read this section already, read it aloud. Otherwise go on to "Questions for Application."

15:1. In Cornelius's conversion, the Holy Spirit worked overtime to reveal God's will. Peter felt compelled to welcome Cornelius and his friends into the Church without circumcision, since God had already welcomed them into Christ without waiting for them to become Jews. But no matter how obvious the Spirit's activity, the Christians still had to deal with the question of whether the baptism of Cornelius and company was a precedent or an anomaly. Did it indicate the pattern the Church should now follow, or was it just an exception to the rule?

The question of admitting Gentiles into the Church without requiring them to become Jews raised profound issues. If Gentiles are saved by belief in Jesus without keeping the Mosaic law, then Jesus rather than the Mosaic law plays the central role in the relationship between God and his people. By defining certain foods, persons, and things as unclean, the Mosaic law erected a wall of ritual purity around those who observed it. If Jesus rather than the Mosaic law is central in the renewed Israel of the Church, then Jesus bridges the separation that is based on ritual regulations.

To many Jewish Christians, this was unthinkable. In their view, the Mosaic law remained central, and gentile converts had to follow it. Although Luke does not say it, these Jewish Christians probably refused to associate with the gentile converts, considering them ritually impure (see 11:1–3; Galatians 2:11–12).

15:2–4. While the Antioch community is large and mature enough to be sending out its own missionaries, the Antioch Christians recognize the mother church in Jerusalem, headed by the apostles, as the central authority for resolving the disagreement. In Jerusalem, "elders" now share in leadership with the apostles. Luke implies that an orderly transfer of authority is underway from the apostles to the next generation of leaders.

15:5. In Jerusalem, some Christians who are Pharisees repeat the demand that the gentile believers become Jews. The fact that Pharisees, who advocated scrupulous observance of the Mosaic law, were attracted to the Christian movement shows that in general the Jerusalem Christians kept the law carefully.

15:6–11. Paul and Barnabas's missionary report is edifying but calls for discernment, which Peter attempts to supply. He briefly recounts the event at Cornelius's house. His concluding remark shows that further reflection has led him to see that Jesus, not the Mosaic law, is the decisive factor in believers' relationship with God. Thus to insist that gentile believers keep the Mosaic law would ignore what God has done through Jesus and the Spirit.

15:12. The assembly receives Peter's argument with silence, indicating agreement. But someone still needs to show how God's present action among the Gentiles connects with what God has already revealed. This is the task of James, a relative of Jesus (see Mark 6:3), who is now the local leader of the Jerusalem community (apparently Peter no longer resides there—12:17).

15:13–21. James draws from Scripture to confirm that what Peter has described fulfills God's long-standing intentions (15:16–18). Consequently, James says, gentile converts should not be required to follow the Mosaic law but merely to—what? Scholars have long debated the meaning of the prohibitions in verse 20. Two main possibilities emerge: (1) James's requirements concern matters of ritual uncleanness that gentile believers should avoid so that Jewish believers can feel comfortable associating with them (the regulations forbid eating non-kosher meat and marrying within too close a degree of relationship), and (2) the requirements prohibit taking part in idolatrous worship (they forbid eating offerings sacrificed to idols and engaging in sexual immorality and other practices associated with pagan ceremonies).

15:22–35. James's decision is ratified by the leaders and the rest of the Church. With Jesus, rather than the Mosaic covenant, at its center, the Church will leave behind Israel's traditional focus on chosen land, temple, law, and national life that grew from that covenant. Centered on Jesus, the Church will bring the gospel to people in *every* land; it will worship God through Jesus and the Spirit equally in *every* place; it will seek a deeper relationship with God not through scrupulous observance of written and oral law but by personal discipleship to Jesus. It will be a community open to incorporating—and transforming—every people and culture.

Questions for Application

40 minutes
Choose questions according to your interest and time.

1 Paul, Barnabas, and Peter were attentive to what the Spirit was doing. How can we identify where God is at work in our lives and in the world around us? What kind of discernment is needed to test our observations? What is the value of talking with others about what we think God is doing?

2 What does it mean to have Jesus at the center of your life? What competes with Jesus for center stage in your life? What could you do to keep your life better focused on Jesus?

3 How could you apply to a disagreement or conflict in your own life some lesson from the early Christians' resolution of their disagreement in this chapter?

4   What personal, social, economic, or ethnic factors act as barriers between members of the Christian community today? Which ones do you experience? What could you do to help overcome one of these barriers?

5   When you have to make an important decision, whom do you consult? What qualities do you look for in someone whose advice you seek?

6   What experience has shown you the value of listening carefully to another person? How has this experience affected you?

"Sharing about the Bible is just that; it is not teaching and being taught."

John Burke, O.P., *Beginners' Guide to Bible Sharing*

Approach to Prayer

15 minutes
Use this approach—or create your own!

✦ Ask God for wisdom to deal with problems in your personal lives, in your parish, in the Church, in your work, in your city, etc.

Pray a Hail Mary together to begin. Take a few minutes either for silent reflection or for participants, if they wish, to mention problems for which they would like the group to pray. Then pray together this prayer, which Byzantine Catholics pray in the liturgy between the Scripture readings and the homily.

Heavenly king, Comforter, Spirit of truth, you are present everywhere and fill all things. Treasury of blessings and giver of life, come and dwell within us, cleanse us of all stain, and save our souls, O gracious Lord.

Saints in the Making

A Constructive Approach to Controversy

This section is a supplement for individual reading.

Those who conducted the council in Jerusalem left future generations of Christians a model for handling disagreement. An early observer to remark on this model was St. John Chrysostom. In the summer of 400, Bishop John preached several homilies on Acts 15 to his congregation in Constantinople (Istanbul). Perhaps the many disputes that troubled the Church of his day sensitized him to the importance of constructive conflict resolution.

John pointed out that in Acts the church leaders did not engage in recriminations. Because the Jewish Christians who had gone to Antioch insisting that gentile converts be circumcised had not been authorized by the Jerusalem church leadership, there were grounds for making accusations against them. Paul and Barnabas, however, "do not show up making accusations, but 'declaring all the things that God had done with them,'" John observed. The Jerusalem leaders, who could have focused on the self-appointed teachers' insubordination, spoke "mildly," John said, "and not with an emphasis on their authority. Such amiable words are more likely to fix themselves in the mind. . . . Notice how they say nothing harsh against the unauthorized teachers but focus on undoing the damage that has been done. . . . They do not call them, 'Seducers!' or 'Pestilent fellows!' or anything like that."

Indeed, John remarked, gentleness characterized the church leaders' entire handling of the disagreement. This was best, John said, for "gentleness is everywhere a great good, while it is impossible for one who is out of temper ever to persuade." The leaders did not throw their weight around, John noted. After Peter spoke, "The entire assembly kept silence. There was no arrogance in the church." While Peter and Paul spoke, no one interrupted; and James, who was in charge, waited patiently. "The orderliness was great because their hearts were free from love of glory!"

Finally, John thought the council was wise to involve both those who were engaged in the controversial activities (Peter, Paul, and Barnabas, who had preached to Gentiles) and someone who was uninvolved (James). James was able to argue dispassionately, without having to worry about defending his actions.

Between Discussions

hoosing six readings from Acts is a frustrating task, because the selection inevitably will be unbalanced. The readings in this booklet are concentrated in the first half of Acts.
As a result the selection is heavy on the church in Jerusalem and
light on the churches in the gentile world.

Another imbalance concerns women. Both men and
women have been present in many of the scenes so far—receiving
the Spirit at Pentecost, listening to Peter's preaching in the temple, embracing the gospel at Cornelius's house. But the individuals
identified by name are almost all men.

In other sections of Acts, however, several women step
out of the anonymous crowd and into the spotlight wearing a name-
tag. Almost all of them play a constructive role in the early Church.
These women do not give the great speeches or head the pioneer
missionary teams. Luke shows them moving within the more ordinary range of Christians' activities of the time. Taking a look at
these women, then, puts us in touch with important aspects of
Christian life "on the ground," as most Christians experienced it.
Here, briefly, are the more important of these women.

Mary (1:13–14). The mother of Jesus is glimpsed sitting
upstairs in a large house in Jerusalem among the followers of Jesus
who are waiting for the Spirit. Her presence must have been an
encouragement to trust in God, for she was a living witness to
God's faithfulness to his promises. Mary's role in the Church was
utterly unique: she was the mother of the Lord. Yet she also filled
the role of model disciple, for she exemplified how every disciple of
the Lord ought to listen for his word, receive it with faith, and be
totally available for his plans (see Luke 1:38; 2:19, 51).

Tabitha (9:36–42). She is a "female disciple" (9:36—
only here in the Greek New Testament is the feminine form of
"disciple" used). She devoted her time and money to caring for
poor people, which shows that she had material means at her dis-
posal. Tabitha responded practically to the gospel by using her
resources to help others. But she did more than write checks; she
gave of herself: the recipients of her generosity show Peter the
clothing she made for them. Tabitha experienced God's action in

a very remarkable way, for after she died, Peter raised her back to life through prayer.

Mary, the mother of John Mark (12:12–17). She too was a woman of means, for she had a home large enough to host meetings of Christians in Jerusalem. While her son John Mark and another relative, Barnabas, went on missionary journeys, Mary remained at home. But she was not cut off from the world. In those days, a variety of activities took place in the homes of more affluent people—business was transacted; goods were made and sold; sick and needy persons were cared for; and relatives, friends, and clients interacted with one another. Mary may have played an important part in many people's lives, not least in the lives of the Christians who met regularly in her home.

Lydia (16:12–40). We read about this businesswoman in Week 6.

Philip's daughters (21:9). Like the martyred Stephen, Philip was one of the seven Greek-speaking Jewish leaders in Jerusalem (6:5). He left Jerusalem and spread the gospel in various places, ending up in Caesarea. His four daughters are mentioned only in passing, but what Luke says about them is significant. Philip's daughters exercised the gift of prophecy. Their role of delivering inspired messages from the Lord would have been greatly valued and may have had a significant effect on the Church, at least if we are to judge from the impact of later prophetic women in the Church, such as St. Catherine of Siena.

Priscilla (18:1–3, 18, 24–26). She and her husband, Aquila, shared their home and their work (making leather tents) with Paul. They also traveled with Paul. When a promising and already well-educated Christian speaker named Apollos showed up in town needing more instruction in the faith, Paul turned him over to Priscilla and Aquila. Because Luke mentions Priscilla before Aquila, it would seem that she played at least an equal part in Apollos's further education. Since Apollos had already obtained an excellent literary and religious education, we can only conclude that Priscilla and her husband were highly educated and reliable Christian teachers.

MISSIONARY ADVENTURES

Questions to Begin

15 minutes
Use a question or two to get warmed up for the reading.

1 Describe a time when you made a hasty judgment about someone and later realized you were mistaken. What were the consequences? What have you learned?

2 When do you sing?
- ☑ When I'm happy.
- ☐ When I'm depressed, to keep my spirits up.
- ☐ Only when I'm alone (in the car? in the shower?).
- ☐ As much as possible.
- ☐ When I'm with other people (with whom? on what occasions?).
- ☐ Only when I'm at church.
- ☐ Never.

5 minutes
Read the passage aloud. Let individuals take turns reading
paragraphs.

The Reading: Acts 15:36–40; 16:8–40

A Missionary Journey

36 After some days Paul said to Barnabas, "Come, let us return and
visit the believers in every city where we proclaimed the word of the
Lord and see how they are doing." 37 Barnabas wanted to take with
them John called Mark. 38 But Paul decided not to take with them one
who had deserted them in Pamphylia and had not accompanied them
in the work. 39 The disagreement became so sharp that they parted
company; Barnabas took Mark with him and sailed away to Cyprus.
40 But Paul chose Silas and set out, the believers commending him to
the grace of the Lord. . . .

16:8 [P]assing by Mysia, they went down to Troas. 9 During
the night Paul had a vision: there stood a man of Macedonia pleading
with him and saying, "Come over to Macedonia and help us." 10
When he had seen the vision, we immediately tried to cross over to
Macedonia, being convinced that God had called us to proclaim the
good news to them.

11 We set sail from Troas and took a straight course to
Samothrace, the following day to Neapolis, 12 and from there to
Philippi, which is a leading city of the district of Macedonia and a
Roman colony. . . . 13 On the sabbath day we went outside the gate
by the river, where we supposed there was a place of prayer; and we
sat down and spoke to the women who had gathered there. 14 A certain woman named Lydia, a worshiper of God, was listening to us;
she was from the city of Thyatira and a dealer in purple cloth. The
Lord opened her heart to listen eagerly to what was said by Paul.
15 When she and her household were baptized, she urged us, saying,
"If you have judged me to be faithful to the Lord, come and stay at
my home." And she prevailed upon us.

The Downs and Ups of Christian Mission

16 One day, as we were going to the place of prayer, we met a slave-
girl who had a spirit of divination and brought her owners a great
deal of money by fortune telling. 17 While she followed Paul and us,
she would cry out, "These men are slaves of the Most High God, who
proclaim to you a way of salvation." 18 . . . But Paul, very much

annoyed, turned and said to the spirit, "I order you in the name of Jesus Christ to come out of her." And it came out that very hour.

19 But when her owners saw that their hope of making money was gone, they seized Paul and Silas and dragged them into the marketplace before the authorities. 20 When they had brought them before the magistrates, they said, "These men are disturbing our city; they are Jews 21 and are advocating customs that are not lawful for us as Romans to adopt or observe." 22 The crowd joined in attacking them, and the magistrates had them stripped of their clothing and ordered them to be beaten with rods. 23 After they had given them a severe flogging, they threw them into prison. . . .

25 About midnight Paul and Silas were praying and singing hymns to God, and the prisoners were listening to them. 26 Suddenly there was an earthquake, so violent that the foundations of the prison were shaken; and immediately all the doors were opened and everyone's chains were unfastened. 27 When the jailer woke up and saw the prison doors wide open, he drew his sword and was about to kill himself, since he supposed that the prisoners had escaped. 28 But Paul shouted in a loud voice, "Do not harm yourself, for we are all here." 29 The jailer called for lights, and rushing in, he fell down trembling before Paul and Silas. 30 Then he brought them outside and said, "Sirs, what must I do to be saved?" 31 They answered, "Believe on the Lord Jesus, and you will be saved, you and your household." 32 They spoke the word of the Lord to him and to all who were in his house. 33 At the same hour of the night he took them and washed their wounds; then he and his entire family were baptized without delay. 34 He brought them up into the house and set food before them; and he and his entire household rejoiced that he had become a believer in God.

35 When morning came, the magistrates sent the police, saying, "Let those men go." . . . 37 But Paul replied, "They have beaten us in public, uncondemned, men who are Roman citizens, and have thrown us into prison; and now are they going to discharge us in secret? Certainly not! Let them come and take us out themselves." 38 The police reported these words to the magistrates, and they were afraid when they heard that they were Roman citizens; 39 so they came and apologized to them. And they took them out and asked them to leave the city. 40 After leaving the prison they went to Lydia's home; and when they had seen and encouraged the brothers and sisters there, they departed.

10 minutes
Choose questions according to your interest and time.

1 Philippi is a Roman settlement. What aspects of Roman law enter into the episodes in this week's reading?

2 Luke says that the Spirit guided Lydia to listen carefully to Paul. In what way was God involved in preparing the jailer to be receptive to Paul's message?

3 What does the location of the Jewish place of prayer (16:13) suggest about the place that Jews occupied in Philippian society? What do verses 20–23 add to the picture of Jews in the city? In light of this, how easy would it have been for the jailer and his household, who were not Jews, to embrace the message of the Jewish Christian missionaries?

4 At what point does Luke begin using "we" and "us"? Where does he seem to be at the beginning of this reading? Where is he at the end?

5 What does this reading tell you about the kind of person Paul was? How is this picture affected by considering also what is said about him in the readings in Weeks 3 and 5?

A Guide to the Reading

If participants have not read this section already, read it aloud. Otherwise go on to "Questions for Application."

15:36–40. Agreement on a tough issue (15:1–29) is soon followed by disagreement over a minor practical matter between two of the most closely associated Christian leaders: Barnabas and Paul, who have worked together for more than a decade (9:27; 11:25–26; 13:1–14:28). Their plan to make pastoral visitations to believers they evangelized is now disrupted by the question of whether to take along John Mark, who abandoned them halfway into the previous trip (13:13). Paul refuses, perhaps concerned that John Mark will leave them up a creek at some dangerous moment. Barnabas seems willing to overlook the risk, possibly because John Mark is his cousin (Colossians 4:10).

Unable to resolve their disagreement, Barnabas and Paul separate. This is the last mention of Barnabas in Acts. Are we to conclude that he placed family loyalties over missionary priorities (compare to Luke 9:62)? Or should we view Paul as inflexible and domineering? Luke leaves us to ponder the interplay of God's Spirit and human personalities. The Church is indeed a mysterious combination of divine and (flawed) human elements. (Philemon 24 implies that Paul and John Mark were later reconciled.)

16:8–12. Paul and Silas travel west through what is now Turkey. When they arrive at the coast, a dream guides them to sail to a region within present-day Greece. Notice the "we" in verse 10. Apparently Luke has joined the missionary team.

16:13–15. Philippi was largely composed of Roman immigrants, with few Jewish residents and no synagogue. It is not clear whether the "place of prayer" was a building for Jewish meetings outside the city or simply an outdoor area for gathering. At the place of prayer, Paul and his friends run into some women, one of whom is Lydia, a well-to-do merchant of dyed fabrics. Luke's statement that "the Lord opened her heart to listen eagerly" nicely balances the action of the Spirit and Lydia's response. The Spirit inspires her to pay attention but does not force her to believe in Jesus; yet she could not believe without the Spirit's help.

16:16–18. The fortune-teller's proclamation that the missionaries represent the "Most High God" and teach a way of "salvation" might seem a welcome confirmation. But listeners could have misunderstood it to mean that the men were agents of *Zeus* bringing *magical healing*.

16:19–24. In the anti-Jewish atmosphere of ancient Mediterranean cities, it was not hard to stir up a crowd against Jews. To soothe the crowd, the magistrates have the out-of-town troublemakers beaten and jailed without bothering to investigate.

16:25–26. Acts contains many descriptions of the Spirit's effect on those who believe in Jesus. Perhaps the most remarkable effects are the Christians' responses to suffering. The imprisoned missionaries' joyful praise of God seems a more powerful manifestation of the Spirit than the earthquake that breaks open the jail.

16:27–34. The jailer may regard Paul and Silas as magicians whose prayers have caused the earthquake. His question may mean, "What can I do to avert your anger?" Paul and Silas, ever ready to seize an opportunity to present the gospel, tell him about Jesus. The jailer is converted on the spot. Before bringing Paul and Silas into his house, he washes their wounds, and he and his household are baptized, perhaps at a well in the courtyard of his residence. John Chrysostom remarks: "He washed them of their wounds, while he himself was washed of his sins."

16:35–39. In Roman settlements such as Philippi, the magistrates had only limited authority to imprison or physically punish Roman citizens, and certainly never without a trial. Why don't Paul and Silas declare their citizenship *before* getting beaten? It is likely that not all the members of the new Christian community are protected by Roman citizenship. Paul might feel that he can hardly encourage them to accept suffering for Christ if he uses his privileges to escape persecution. A concern for the converts might also underlie Paul's insistence that the magistrates admit their mistake. If the magistrates are publicly shamed for their attack on the missionaries, they might be inclined to leave the other Christians alone.

16:40. Lydia's house has become the meeting place and center of the Philippian church, a crucial service for a community that has no legal recognition—or church building.

Questions for Application

40 minutes
Choose questions according to your interest and time.

1 When has a chance encounter with someone helped you come closer to God? When has a chance encounter given you an opportunity to communicate about God's love with another person? How did you use the opportunity?

2 For some people, disagreements within the Church are an obstacle to believing that the Church is the body of Christ. Do you feel this way? Consider the incidents in 15:1–29 and 15:36–40 when answering this question.

3 The gospel came to Lydia and the jailer in different ways, one rather ordinary, the other extraordinary. How has the gospel come to you? What experience showed you that God knows how to shape his communication with you in a way that fits your personality and needs?

4 The girl's prophetic announcement was open to misunderstanding (16:17). In what ways
do Christians and non-Christians
today sometimes use the same
words to mean different things?
What aspects of the Christian
message are especially open to
misunderstanding today?

5 Think of a situation in which
you suffered unfairly because
of your efforts to be of service.
How would you compare your
response to that of Paul and
Silas in 16:25? Read 2
Corinthians 1:3–11, in which
Paul describes his experience
of persecution on another
occasion. How does it fit
together with the picture in
16:25? What can you learn
from each of these passages?

**"Be conversational. The group is not a place for impressive
theological prayers. Keep prayer relaxed and relational. Be brief."**

Jeffrey Arnold, *Seven Tools for Building Effective Groups*

Approach to Prayer

15 minutes
Use this approach—or create your own!

✦ Ask someone to read aloud this excerpt from Vatican Council's *The Decree on the Apostolate of the Laity* (section 3).

The Christian mission is carried out in the faith, hope, and love that the Holy Spirit pours into the hearts of all the members of the Church. Yes indeed, by the command to love, all the faithful are driven to act for God's glory through the coming of his kingdom and for eternal life for all people, so that they might know the only true God and the one he has sent, Jesus Christ. . . . Therefore, on all the faithful is placed the noble burden of laboring so that the divine announcement of salvation might be known and received by all people everywhere in the world.

If your group wanted to make the Lord known, what would you need? Let people make suggestions, and after each one the group can pray, "Empower us by your Spirit, O Lord." End together with the Our Father.

Saints in the Making

Grace at Pentecost

This section is a supplement for individual reading.

Louise de Marillac's husband was ill, the couple faced financial difficulties, and she was adrift on a dark sea of guilt and doubt. Louise loved her husband, Antoine, yet she was afraid that she had offended God by marrying after previously deciding to enter the convent. Religious doubts assailed her: Is there any life after death? Is there really a God?

People close to Louise gave her good advice. A bishop friend assured her that "serenity will return to you after the storm clouds" clear away. An uncle advised her to let go of her own plans for her life and to receive from God with humility and gratitude whatever he wished to give her. But at the feast of the Ascension in 1623, she was approaching the brink of despair. No efforts of her own, no prayer, seemed to help.

But then, ten days later, during Mass on Pentecost, God spoke to her. He removed her sense of guilt about marrying and indicated that in the future a new opportunity for the kind of religious life to which she had earlier aspired would open up. He also guided her to a new spiritual director. The very clarity of God's voice in her heart overcame her doubts.

This Pentecost experience renewed Louise's relationship with God, but a painful period followed. Antoine died. Louise's financial problems worsened. Louise's situation as a widow, however, gave her a new freedom, and a priest named Vincent de Paul helped her discern what God wanted her to do with it. Vincent was the leader of a movement to provide basic necessities to destitute people such as orphans and prisoners. Louise began to work with him.

Each year, Louise used the days from Ascension to Pentecost as a special time of retreat and prayer. The Pentecost season, filled with an awareness of the action of the Spirit, was always a particularly happy and fruitful time for her.

For more than thirty years Louise and Vincent cooperated in organizing a growing number of French women and men for service to the poor. Their slogan was "The poor are Jesus Christ." Through religious orders—the Vincentians and the Sisters of Charity—and the St. Vincent de Paul Society, an association of laypeople, Vincent and Louise's efforts to care for the neediest people continue today.

After Words

After the episode at Philippi, Paul remains the focus of the rest of Acts. Rather than giving us a list of cities to which Christianity spread and figures on the number of people who were baptized, Luke relates the growth of the Church by following Paul's travels and church-founding, his arrest, imprisonment, shipwreck, and continued preaching. Luke's way of recording the Church's early history reminds us that ultimately it is not programs or institutions that communicate the gospel, but men and women.

17–20. From Philippi, Paul and his companions travel through present-day Greece and western Turkey. In each city Paul preaches in the synagogue, where he has a chance to speak about Messiah Jesus to Jews and Gentiles who, like Cornelius, are admirers of Judaism. In city after city some Jews and "God-fearing" Gentiles accept the gospel, but sooner or later other Jews gang up on Paul and drive him out of town. The reader marvels at Paul's persistence.

In addition, Paul preaches to Gentiles who have no connection with Judaism. This brings some men and women to faith in Christ, but it also lands Paul in deep trouble with the advocates of the various polytheistic religions. In Ephesus, Paul's activities spark a massive riot by people who earn a living from pilgrims who visit the immense shrine in Ephesus to the goddess Artemis. They are afraid that conversions to Christianity will cut into their business.

Paul's experience sets the pattern for later developments. As the Christian community emerges from its matrix in Judaism, Christian missionaries spend less time attempting to convince Jews that Jesus is the Messiah and more time persuading polytheistic Gentiles that there is really only one God and Jesus is his Son. As Christians increasingly address themselves to Gentiles, the problem of sporadic persecution by Jewish authorities will diminish while organized repression from the pagan Roman government will grow, culminating in systematic persecutions in the third and early fourth centuries.

21–22. Paul turns east, hoping to celebrate Pentecost in Jerusalem. As he sails from city to city, visiting groups of disciples along the way, some Christians are inspired by the Spirit to warn him that danger awaits him in the holy city. Sure enough, when Paul gets to Jerusalem a misunderstanding occurs and a riot breaks out in the temple. Paul is about to be killed when the Roman military intervene and put him in protective custody.

23–28. For the remainder of Acts, Paul is under arrest. He is questioned in Jerusalem and at Caesarea, the Romans' provincial capital in Palestine. The Roman authorities do not wish to anger the Jewish leaders in Jerusalem, and so they allow the case to drag on without resolution for a couple of years.

Finally Paul exercises his right as a Roman citizen to have the case transferred to a Roman court. The governor sends Paul under guard by sea to Rome. Not all is smooth sailing, however, and the ship is lost in a storm. Paul and the other passengers barely survive. Luke's account is not only one of the greatest sea stories to come to us from the ancient world; it also lets us see Paul as a spiritual man who has a humane sense of solidarity with his guards and fellow passengers.

Acts ends on what may seem like a dissatisfying note. Paul is under house arrest in Rome. We are not told whether his case ever comes to trial or, if it does, what the outcome is. Is Paul released to continue his missionary work? Is he found guilty? If so, of what crime? With what punishment?

Not surprisingly, there has been a lot of debate about this ending. Some scholars wonder whether Luke's original conclusion has been lost. But others argue that this is indeed how Luke brought his work to a close. Jesus had commissioned his followers to make him known from Jerusalem to the ends of the earth (1:8). In the final scene of Acts 28, Luke shows that the gospel has moved from Jerusalem to the center of the political and cultural world of the day. Now it is up to Luke's readers to carry out the rest of the commission and bring the gospel to the ends of the world.

One of my favorite magazine names is that chosen by a renewal movement among American Episcopalians: *Acts 29.* Luke's Acts ends at chapter 28. The "twenty-ninth chapter" is the chapter of the acts of you and me, in service to Jesus Christ.

You Shall Receive Power

The Main Character in Acts
Is Known through His Impact on People

At the beginning of his public ministry, after being baptized by John the Baptist, Jesus returned to Galilee and began to announce that the kingdom of God was about to arrive (Mark 1:14–15). People saw him as he walked along the lakeshore. They heard his voice. If they were near him in the synagogue on the Sabbath, they felt and smelled him. His disciples ate meals with him and slept in the same room with him at Peter's house in Capernaum. None of this was in the least remarkable. Jesus was "one in being with the Father," as we affirm in the creed, yet he was also a human being.

By contrast, when the Holy Spirit came to Jesus' disciples on Pentecost, they experienced phenomena—a noise like wind, a brightness like fire—but the Spirit himself could not be seen or heard. The Spirit was not incarnated as Jesus was, and thus could not be directly observed. He could be known only through the effects that he produced.

In a sense, as Jesus is the main character in the Gospels, the Holy Spirit is the main character in Acts. But we have to read Acts differently from the Gospels to follow the main character. In the Gospels, the main character is before our eyes. In Acts, we must discover the main character through his impact.

Fortunately this is not difficult to do. Luke has made the dots fairly prominent, and it is not too hard to connect them into a sketch of the Spirit at work in the early Church. The early chapters of Acts are filled with easily detectable signs of the Spirit. Here are some that I notice. What others can you discover?

Peter became courageous. Earlier, despite his best intentions, Peter acted as a coward (Luke 22:33, 54–62). After the Spirit came, he spoke about Jesus publicly and boldly, without concern for his own safety (2:14; 4:8–20; 5:27–32, 40–42).

People who had rejected Jesus accepted him. When Peter spoke in the power of the Spirit, some of the very people who had demanded Jesus' execution came to believe that he is the Messiah (Luke 23:18–23; Acts 2:37–42; 3:13–17; 4:4).

The apostles grasped how God is working in these "last days." During his ministry, Jesus' closest followers had expected him to lead the national liberation of Israel. They had continued to nurse this hope even after he rose from the dead (1:6). With the coming of the Spirit, they comprehended that, instead of "restoring the kingdom to Israel," God is offering his Spirit to men and women to bring them into unity with himself and one another (2:38–39, 43–47).

Jesus' disciples became united in love and service. Once the Spirit came, the group of Jesus' followers evolved from a squabbling band of rivals (Luke 9:46; 22:24) into a community marked by extraordinary mutual care.

At this point, you may wish to pause and formulate a picture of the Holy Spirit. From the evidence of his actions in Acts, what kind of person do you conceive the Spirit to be? What are the Spirit's concerns? How does he relate to people? Luke's account suggests many lines of reflection on the Spirit. I myself am particularly struck by a couple of the Spirit's characteristics:

1. The Spirit continues Jesus' work, with a multiplier effect. Peter had been with Jesus day after day for months, even years, listening to his teaching and receiving his direction. Yet some weakness in him remained unchanged. It was the Spirit that empowered Peter to be the man Jesus called him to be.

Jesus had attracted crowds with his miracles and preaching. But the community of committed followers that he left behind was small: only 120 disciples were gathered in Jerusalem (1:15). By contrast, after Peter's Spirit-filled preaching on Pentecost, three thousand people committed their lives to Jesus (2:41).

Jesus had patiently taught his followers about the kingdom of mercy and humble service that he came to bring. But even the inner circle of his disciples did not grasp his message. No matter how many times he corrected them, they continued to look forward to occupying prominent positions when Jesus began to rule. The Spirit, however, transformed these ambitious men into a group of servant leaders able to guide others in a community life marked by mutual love.

The point of these comparisons is not to diminish Jesus but to highlight the Spirit. The Spirit's action depended on what

Jesus had accomplished. The Spirit came only after Jesus died and rose. Yet we cannot help being impressed by how powerfully the Spirit built on Jesus' accomplishment. The Spirit completed things that Jesus had only begun. Jesus told the disciples that it was good for them that he was going away, because only then would the Spirit come. Then they would do greater things than he had done (John 14:12; 16:7). We see Jesus' words beginning to be fulfilled in the opening chapters of Acts.

I suspect that for many of us, our worries and distractions, desire for comfortable routines, and plain lack of faith may make us insensitive to the Spirit's presence. Our awareness of the Spirit may be faint. But we have cause to hope. The Spirit is among us today, no less than he was among the first Christians. He can act powerfully to complete what Jesus has begun in our lives. Perhaps he is simply waiting for us to tell him that it's okay for him to shake up our lives (older spiritual writers called it surrender and trust), so that we too will experience the impact of his presence.

2. The Spirit turns each of us outward—to each other and to the world. Like a magnet attracting metal filaments, the Spirit reorients us toward serving one another and carrying out Christ's mission to the world.

Luke shows us that new believers became suddenly willing to look beyond their private and family interests and to expend their time and money to care for the destitute among them (2:44–45; 4:32–37). Obviously, helping widows and orphans was not a path to advancement or a way to make one's own life more comfortable or secure. This was an expression of love.

The apostles were willing, even glad, to endure the beatings and imprisonments that came their way as they preached the gospel (5:40–41; 16:25). This sprang from their deep desire for men and women to experience God's grace through Jesus.

This is not to say that self-interest disappeared from the Christian community, as we see from the incident with Ananias and Sapphira (5:1–11). Missionaries did not always get along with each other (15:36–39). But a powerful dynamic was at work, overcoming the Christians' deep-seated tendency to look out for their own interests. This was the Holy Spirit. The Spirit placed within the first Christians a love for one another and a desire to see God's kingdom extended in the world.

Luke does not explore the inner transformation that the Spirit accomplishes as he guides the soul on the journey toward God. That task would fall to later spiritual writers, like St. John of the Cross and St. Teresa of Ávila. But Luke shows us very clearly the fundamental direction of the Spirit's action in us: outward, away from self, toward neighbor, and toward God. The Spirit attunes us to the needs of others and to the tempo of God's action. From the Spirit we receive the freedom to put our own interests second to the needs of other people. We are enabled to pray the Our Father with real longing: "May your kingdom come, may your will be done, on earth as in heaven."

This understanding of the Spirit's action gives us a vital clue for how to connect with his power. If we wish to experience the Spirit, we should get into what the Spirit is doing. If the Spirit is engaged in deepening the community of love among the members of the Church and bringing the light of Christ into the world, we might expect to experience the Spirit working in us as we seek to develop our abilities to serve within the Church and take part in the Church's mission. In other words, the more we bring our lives into line with what the Spirit is doing, the more we may expect to experience his gifts and graces.

Perhaps Peter discovered his new boldness only when he stood up to speak to the crowd on Pentecost morning. Perhaps some of the Christians in Jerusalem realized how greatly they loved one another only when they sold their property and brought the proceeds to the apostles for distribution to the needy brothers and sisters. Perhaps Paul discovered how deeply he wanted God's kingdom to come only on the night when he sat in a dark jail in Philippi and found himself singing praises to God.

If we start moving in the direction in which the Spirit wants us to move, we can be sure that we will experience his power helping us along the way.

Other Ways of Saying *Church*

In Acts, Luke often writes about the Church without using the Greek word for *church* (in our readings he only uses it in 8:1, 3; 15:3, 4, 22). Instead he uses descriptive terms, such as "the whole group of those who believed" (4:32) and "the whole community of the disciples" (6:2). These alternative ways of speaking about the Church give us much to ponder about our identity as the group of Jesus' followers today. Here are a few.

1. "My witnesses." Before Pentecost, Jesus tells his followers that when the Spirit comes, "You will be my witnesses in Jerusalem, in all Judea and Samaria, and to the ends of the earth" (1:8). This statement sets the agenda for Acts, which chronicles the Church's growth from a gathering of Jewish men and women in a house in Jerusalem to a network of Jewish-gentile communities spread across the Roman empire.

Jesus' words set an agenda for our lives too. "You shall be my witnesses." His words impel us to ask ourselves how well our lives reflect him to other people. Do people experience his humility and compassion when they come in contact with us? What is there about our lives that might lead others to conclude that we believe that Jesus is the risen Lord? Do we articulate our faith in Jesus for others so that they have a chance to come to know him?

2. "The disciples." Luke speaks often of the "community of the disciples" (6:2) and more often simply of "the disciples" (in our readings: 9:1, 19, 26; 15:10). Unlike mere students, disciples have a close relationship with their master. To call the Christian movement a community of disciples means that it is composed of men and women each of whom has a one-on-one relationship with Jesus. Further, disciples are not just companions; they are learners. The Church, then, is a community of learners. No one has arrived at perfection; but neither is anyone free to drift along without learning and changing. Each of us is on a program of transformation with the help of our personal trainer, Jesus. Do you think of yourself as a disciple of Jesus?

3. Those who "belonged to the Way" (9:2). This suggests that the Church is on a road to God, and that its members follow a way of life together. What does it mean to lead your life as a pilgrimage toward God? What aspect of your life is Jesus calling you to reshape to fit his way of living?

4. "Brothers and sisters." Luke often refers to groups of Christians as "brothers" (for example, 10:23; 15:1, 3, 22, 23, 32, 33, 36, 40; 16:40), and Christians often address each other as "brothers" (9:17; 15:7, 13). (To avoid using a masculine word for both men and women, the NRSV often renders the Greek word for *brothers* as "believers" or "friends," words that fail to convey the followers' familial bond. At 16:40, however, the NRSV translates the word with the phrase "brothers and sisters.")

In ancient times, the family held life together. In a dangerous world without social security systems, people depended on their relatives. To acknowledge a person as brother or sister was to recognize a commitment. Jesus called his followers to commit their whole lives to him; this, in turn, brought them into a relationship with one another. Jesus described the result in terms of family: "Looking at those who sat around him, he said, 'Here are my mother and my brothers! Whoever does the will of God is my brother and sister and mother'" (Mark 3:34–35).

After Pentecost, Jesus' followers continued to recognize each other as brothers and sisters. By creating smaller groupings of fellow disciples, such as home-based groupings, and by establishing distinct sections of the community for different language groups (2:46; 6:1–7), the followers made it possible for members to maintain a familial relationship with each other, even as the community grew to thousands of members.

To what degree do you and others in your local church family demonstrate a familial kind of affection, trust, care, and commitment to each other? Would it be helpful to develop smaller groupings within the church to enable members to know and care for each other? (Perhaps your own Bible discussion group is already a step in this direction!)

5. The "fellowship" (2:42). The Greek word translated "fellowship" in 2:42 is *koinonía*. Joseph Fitzmyer translates it "a communal form of life" and remarks that it "is the first way that Luke names the Christian church in Acts." *Koinonía* means sharing or participating in something together. The Christians shared in the apostles' message about Jesus and in the Spirit; that sharing generated a fellowship, or community, with one another (see the *Catechism of the Catholic Church,* section 813).

6. Those who "had all things in common" (2:44). Because they shared in the life of God together, the believers also shared their material resources with each other.

Luke does not give us details on how exactly the Christians in Jerusalem did this. Apparently the sharing was voluntary (5:4). In the view of some scholars, the sharing involved eating daily meals together, rather than simply a distribution of funds (the Greek text of 2:46; 6:1 speaks literally of "daily ministry," not "daily distribution"). In other words, the material sharing involved a real sharing of life. Wealthier and poorer members of the community were drawn into a relationship with each other that they would not have had without the community.

This example spurs us to examine our own situations and evaluate the care that we offer one another. Many parishes have a St. Vincent de Paul Society or other mechanisms for identifying and meeting the needs of those in the parish. How well do such arrangements work in your parish? What efforts could you make so that in your parish also the words, "There was not a needy person among them" (4:34) would be fulfilled? Do wealthier and poorer members of your parish treat each other as brothers and sisters? Do they ever share meals together?

7. The renewed community of Israel. Luke does not use this term, but it is present in his mind and in the minds of the apostles, as we can see from an incident after Jesus' ascension. Jesus had chosen twelve of his disciples to function as an inner group. One of them, Judas, abandoned his place by betraying Jesus. While Jesus' followers waited for the Spirit, Peter guided them in choosing a replacement for Judas (1:15–26). Peter thought it was important for the group of twelve to be at full strength for launching the Church, because that number helped express what the Church is. Twelve was the number of tribes that traditionally constituted Israel. Thus the twelve apostles symbolized that the disciples were the renewed people of Israel gathered around Israel's Messiah.

The Church began not as a replacement of Israel, let alone a separate religion, but as the renewal of Israel. Since those early days, Christianity and Judaism have gone separate ways, sometimes with animosity. But in the Church, which began as the renewed community of Israel and believes that its Lord is the Jewish Messiah, prejudice toward Jews and Judaism can be only a perverse aberration. Vatican Council II says that "the church . . . mindful of her common patrimony with the Jews . . . deplores . . . anti-Semitism directed against the Jews at any time and from any source" (*Declaration on the Relationship of the Church to Non-Christian Religions,* section 4). True, the gospel encountered opposition in first-century Judaism. But to the Jewish Christians such as Peter and John who faced this opposition, the idea of "Christian anti-Semitism" would have seemed an absurd self-contradiction.

8. "Me" (9:4, 16). Speaking to Paul, Jesus refers to the members of the Church who are suffering persecution for him as parts of himself: "Why do you persecute *me*?" (italics mine). The members of the Church are joined to Christ not in an extrinsic way, like gloves, but in an intrinsic way, like hands. Jesus in heaven is profoundly united with his followers on earth.

This has many implications (Paul develops some in 1 Corinthians 6:12–20; 12:12–31). Jesus' words in Acts 9:16 specifically concern the sharing of suffering between himself and his followers. His words suggest that we might call the Church "the community of those who share in Jesus' suffering."

Are you and I willing to offer our sufferings to God, in union with Jesus, for the advancement of his kingdom in the world (see Colossians 1:24)? Will we share in the Church's work in the world, even when it becomes difficult and painful (see Romans 8:17; Philippians 3:10)? As fellow members of the body of Christ, let us pray for each other that our answer will be yes!

Suggestions for Bible Discussion Groups

Like a camping trip, a Bible discussion group works best if you agree on what you're undertaking together, why you're doing it, where you hope to get to, and how you intend to get there. Many groups use their first meeting to consider such questions. Here is a checklist of issues, with a few bits of advice from people with experience in Bible discussions. (A planning discussion will go more smoothly if the leaders have thought through the following issues beforehand.)

Agree on your purpose. Are you getting together to gain wisdom and direction for your life? to finally get acquainted with the Bible? to support one another in following Christ? to encourage those who are exploring—or reexploring—the Church? for other reasons?

Agree on attitudes. For example: "We're all beginners here." "We're here to help each other understand and respond to God's Word." "We're not here to offer counseling or direction to each other." "We want to read Scripture prayerfully." What do *you* wish to emphasize? Make it explicit!

Agree on ground rules. Barbara J. Fleischer, in her useful book *Facilitating for Growth,* recommends that a group clearly state its approach to the following:

+ Preparation. Do we agree to read the material before each meeting?

+ Attendance. What kind of priority will we give to our meetings?

+ Self-revelation. Are we willing to help the others in the group gradually get to know us—our weaknesses as well as our strengths, our needs as well as our gifts?

+ Listening. Will we commit ourselves to listening to each other?

+ Confidentiality. Will we keep everything that is shared with the group in the group?

+ Encouragement and support. Will we give as well as receive?

+ Participation. Will we work to allow everyone time and opportunity to make a contribution?

You could probably take a pen and draw a circle around *listening* and *confidentiality.* Those two points are especially important.

The following items could be added to Fleischer's list:

+ Relationship with parish. Is our group part of the religious education program? independent but operating with the express approval of the pastor? not a parish-based group at all?

+ New members. In the course of the six meetings, will new members be allowed?

Agree on housekeeping.

+ When will we meet?

+ How often will we meet? Meeting weekly or every other week is best if you can manage it. William Riley remarks, "Meetings once a month are too distant from each other for the threads of the last session not to be lost" (*The Bible Study Group: An Owner's Manual*).

+ How long will meetings run?

+ Where will we meet?

+ Is any setup needed? Christine Dodd writes that "the problem with meeting in a place like a church hall is that it can be very soul-destroying" given the cold, impersonal feel of many church facilities. If you have to meet in a church facility, Dodd recommends doing something to make the area homey (*Making Scripture Work*).

+ Who will host the meetings? Leaders and hosts are not necessarily the same.

+ Will we have refreshments? Who will provide them?

+ What about childcare? Most experienced leaders of Bible discussion groups discourage bringing infants or other children to adult Bible discussions.

Agree on leadership. You need someone to facilitate—to keep the discussion on track, to see that everyone has a chance to speak, to help the group stay on schedule. Rena Duff, editor of the newsletter *Sharing God's Word Today,* recommends having two or three people take turns leading the discussions.

It's okay if the leader is not an expert regarding the Bible. You have this booklet, and if questions come up that no one can answer, you can delegate a participant to do a little research between meetings. It's important for the leader to set an example of listening, to draw out the quieter members (and occasionally restrain the more vocal ones), to move the group on when it gets stuck, to remind the members of their agreements, and to summarize what the group is accomplishing.

Bible discussion is an opportunity to experience the fulfillment of Jesus' promise "Where two or three are gathered in my name, I am there among them" (Matthew 18:20). Put your discussion group in Jesus' hands. Pray for the guidance of the Spirit. And have a great time exploring God's Word together!

You can use this booklet just as well for individual study as for group discussion. While discussing the Bible with other people can be a rich experience, there are advantages to individual reading. For example:

+ You can focus on the points that interest you most.

+ You can go at your own pace.

+ You can be completely relaxed and unashamedly honest in your answers to all the questions, since you don't have to share them with anyone else!

My suggestions for using this booklet on your own are these:

+ Don't skip "Questions to Begin." The questions can help you as an individual reader warm up to the topic of the reading.

+ Take your time on "Questions for Careful Reading" and "Questions for Application." While a group will probably not have enough time to work on all the questions, you can allow yourself the time to consider all of them if you are using the booklet by yourself.

+ If you are going through Acts at your own pace, consider reading the entire book, not just the parts excerpted in this booklet. "Between Discussions" pages will give you some guidance in reading the additional portions of Acts. Your total understanding of Luke's account will be greatly increased by reading through Acts from beginning to end.

+ Since you control the pace, give yourself plenty of opportunities to reflect on the meaning of Acts for you. Let your reading be an opportunity for Luke's words to become God's words to you.

Bibles

The following editions of the Bible contain the full set of biblical books recognized by the Catholic Church, along with a great deal of useful explanatory material:

✦ The Catholic Study Bible (Oxford University Press), which uses the text of the New American Bible

✦ The Catholic Bible: Personal Study Edition (Oxford University Press), which also uses the text of the New American Bible

✦ The New Jerusalem Bible, the regular (not the standard or reader's) edition (Doubleday)

Books

✦ Joseph A. Fitzmyer, S.J., *The Acts of the Apostles,* The Anchor Bible, vol. 31 (New York: Doubleday, 1998).

✦ James D. G. Dunn, *The Acts of the Apostles,* Narrative Commentaries (Valley Forge, Pa.: Trinity Press International, 1996).

✦ Ben Witherington III, *The Acts of the Apostles: A Socio-Rhetorical Commentary* (Grand Rapids, Mich.: William B. Eerdmans Publishing Co., 1998).

✦ Luke Timothy Johnson, *The Acts of the Apostles,* Sacra Pagina Series, vol. 5 (Collegeville, Minn.: Liturgical Press, 1992).

How has Scripture had an impact on your life? Was this booklet helpful to you in your study of the Bible? Please send comments, suggestions, and personal experiences to Kevin Perrotta c/o Trade Editorial Department, Loyola Press, 3441 N. Ashland Ave., Chicago, IL 60657.